COMMON SENSE
IN GUIDANCE

Homer P. Gammons

No Longer Property of
Phillips Memorial Library

PHILLIPS MEMORIAL
LIBRARY
PROVIDENCE COLLEGE

**PARKER PUBLISHING
COMPANY, INC.**

West Nyack, N. Y.

LB
1620.5
G24

To My Father

Second Printing.....April, 1970

© 1969 BY

PARKER PUBLISHING COMPANY, INC.

WEST NYACK, N.Y.

ALL RIGHTS RESERVED. NO PART OF THIS
BOOK MAY BE REPRODUCED IN ANY FORM
OR BY ANY MEANS, WITHOUT PERMISSION
IN WRITING FROM THE PUBLISHER

LIBRARY OF CONGRESS
CATALOG CARD NUMBER: 69-15048

PRINTED IN THE UNITED STATES OF AMERICA

B&P

A Note from the Author ...

I suppose it's largely my imagination, but it seems to me that, during twenty years of guidance, I have been at one time or another the unwary victim of every ill-conceived idea and illusion known to the rapidly developing field of guidance. Most of these errors were committed during the lean, tanned years when I was sure of everything. Now, bloody but still battling, I marvel at the wisdom of that earlier Gammons. I have discovered the existence of so many shades of gray! Despite the realization that no one has all the answers, I do have strong convictions about my work which I would like to share in the hope that I might save other fresh, young gladiators from the numerous pitfalls that liberally dot the guidance field. At least, this is my intention and is the primary purpose of this book—to extend a helping hand to those entering a profession that is the most challenging, stimulating and rewarding in the field of education.

I am motivated also by the strong feeling that there is much confusion among counselors already in the field as to the nature and purpose of guidance. I think this is due to the difference in guidance as described in the textbook and guidance as it is, or has to be, practiced in the average school. The textbook naturally concerns itself with ideal situations and theory. This is probably good in that it engenders an awareness of the scope of guidance and the complexities of human behavior. But for many who are thrust into the realities of counseling, there remains a need for a working philosophy, a course of action, a practical point of view. I herewith offer this point of view.

I speak not as an "expert" but as a fellow counselor who has had time to observe and evaluate the efforts of himself and his colleagues. My experience has been largely in a small "middle class" city. It is probably quite representative of most high schools and so, I imagine, are most of its guidance problems. Westfield High School is a 1,000-pupil comprehensive high school. Our student body is truly heterogeneous in that there are wide variations in our students' cultural backgrounds and abilities. Westfield itself is a fortunate blend of urban-rural environments. We have children of factory workers and farmers. We are a rather conservative town, conscious of our colonial past and still clinging to the cultural values of our New England forebears. A large segment of fine second- and third-generation families reinforces this conservatism.

Granted that all schools are different, I believe the reader would find much in Westfield High School with which to identify. If I refer to it from time to time, I do so with the knowledge that Westfield High is not *the* model school. It is a good school, but it has its share of problems (like most high schools), and I will use it mainly because it is a convenient and representative example.

This book is not a scholarly, definitive work on guidance theory and techniques. On the contrary, it will be concerned with many items never discussed in a standard text. It will be a collection of suggestions, observations, and occasional advice. Some of what I say may be considered heresy. In fact, I have been accused by some of my associates of being anti-guidance. If this makes you nervous, take heart in the knowledge that I'm a gentle, harmless fellow and have never taken part in a protest march in my life. We will not use such words as "meaningful," "sibling rivalry" or even "peer acceptance."

For the parents of your students, whose contact with guidance services may be limited to occasional parents' nights, failure notices, and other dismal reminders of their children's inadequacies, I will try to help you by giving them an overview of what guidance is trying to do for their children. This may help us clarify the purpose and limitations of the effective guidance program in the hope that we, in partnership with parents, may cooperate in helping the child make the most of the high school years.

To all the grizzled veterans of guidance, I ask your indulgence and hope that, while you may not agree with me all the way, you will find an occasional helpful idea—and an echo to your own thoughts.

Most of all, I would hope that it will stimulate the kind of personal reassessment that is so vital to all of us in education.

Homer P. Gammons

Contents

1

Analyzing the Role of the Counselor

Freud, God, or Professional Nice Guy?

Twenty years ago, when guidance programs first started to gain wide acceptance, the concept of guidance was very unsophisticated. Vocational choice, testing, job placement and other "helping" services were the usual fare at the guidance training table. There was a great deal of experimentation, as well as a wide variety of programs—from homeroom programs to extensive group guidance classes.

The profession has progressed since then, and there is more unanimity among the experts as to the organization and nature of a guidance program. The counselor has emerged as a respected professional, a necessary member of the team.

Meanwhile, the theoreticians, quite properly, have advanced their research accordingly. Indeed, the literature of today bears little resemblance to that of my graduate training days.

First, an imposing and esoteric vocabulary has developed. Although much of it is necessary, I must admit that I am irked by excessive educational verbiage. There must be a simpler way!

Secondly, much attention today is given to the psychological aspect of counseling. Counselors are frequently referred to as therapists and their counselees as clients. I accept this within the limitations of my own concept of guidance. But I believe it has contributed to an apparent confusion in the minds of many counselors as to the nature of guidance and, in particular, to the role of the counselor in the average high school.

To illustrate my point with a specific example, consider an article selected from *Counseling: Readings in Theory and Practice* [1] which is, incidentally, a highly interesting work of unquestioned merit. Entitled *Behavior Theories and a Counseling Case,* one symposium describes a mythical case of a maladjusted high school boy and offers four analyses and their corresponding solutions as proposed by a "Neo-analyst," a disciple of the Stimulus-Response Reinforcement School, a proponent of the General Behavior Systems theory and the client-centered position of Carl Rogers. Each attacks the problem from his own point of view, and it makes for fascinating reading. But the danger does exist that, after exposure to this or countless other articles written in a psychological vein, the counselor will feel it incumbent upon him to act the role of the psychologist. Filled with Freudian fervor, he may embark on a giddy trip into the wild blue yonder—never to get his feet back on solid ground.

As counselors, we should be well versed in current theory. It should serve as a useful reservoir of ideas for action. But we must interpret theory in the light of the practical limitations imposed by the realities of the average high school. In short, we must make up our minds at the very outset whether we are going to be counselors or psychologists. We can't be both!

We do need psychological services badly in the schools. But to expect that the counselor play two roles—to act as psychologist in any effective clinical manner and to act as a high school counselor, as I understand the role—is unrealistic.

At the same time, I hear the charge from teachers and laymen that counselors are merely professional nice guys. There is a danger that, in avoiding conflict in our relations with our counselees,

---

1 John F. McGowan and Lyle D. Schmidt, *Counseling: Readings in Theory and Practice* (New York, N.Y.: Holt, Rinehart & Winston, Inc., 1962).

we overdo the process of "gaining rapport." However, although counselors should not act as judges, they can certainly be referees. We should not be permissive. Certainly wrong is wrong, stupidity is stupidity, and there is nothing in the book that says the counselor must side with a pupil who is obviously out of line in either his attitudes or behavior. Much of the current resentment of guidance by teachers (and I'll wager it exists in every school in varying degrees—including my own) can be laid to this kind of counselor attitude. We work within an authoritarian situation. I do feel a school should be authoritarian and, while we should *usually* avoid being authoritative ourselves, we are obligated to do everything in our power to reinforce this authority.

Nor is the guidance counselor God. We are just another cog in the machinery of the school. We are part of the teaching mechanism—not apart from it. We should exert ourselves in aiding the teachers to do the most important job in the school—teaching. To the extent that we impede this function, to that extent we fail in our ultimate goal. To those professionals who are impatient with the traditional auxiliary function of guidance and would give it a more independent role, I maintain they are unrealistic and apparently unfamiliar with the way a high school works. I see too many instances of guidance programs that have become well-organized empires, but are divorced from the classroom and, in rare cases, from the whole business of learning.

I realize all this has an unsophisticated ring to it. I hope I don't sound petulant, and I certainly don't mean to be overly critical. I'm confident that most guidance programs do a good job, and the undedicated counselor is a rare bird indeed. Nor do I have a quarrel with professionals at the college level who are quite properly involved in experimentation and theory. It's the application of this theory that bothers me. It boils down to a matter of emphasis, a point of view.

Need for guidance

It has been a long recognized fact of life that the period of adolescence encompasses some of the most miserable days in the life span of man—miserable for parents, for society, and for the teenager himself. I should know. I've just been through it with one daughter and have twin girls coming along—a prospect which

I view with about as much equanimity as I would the invasion of Attila the Hun.

In the old days, we happily lumped these hormone-stricken youngsters together, exposed them to reading, writing, and the junior prom, naturally assuming some of them would eventually graduate and take their positions in the adult world. Except for the occasional perceptive teacher and principal, these children received little educational or vocational guidance during their transition from child to adult—except from Aunt Hattie (who had been to college) and Uncle Ed (who knew the boss at the local shoe factory).

Now the adult world is more complex and much more frightening. In consequence, there is a need for a special program which can help the high school student understand his potential and his limitations—and point out those myriad opportunities within his capabilities. This program helps the child—soon to become an adult—chart a course, based on this self-knowledge, that will make the entrance into the adult world easier, more profitable, and more satisfying. Such a program, in a sense, is the catalyst that jells the work of the classroom teacher and gives it substance and meaning. However, unlike a chemical catalyst, the counselor who implements the guidance program does not remain unchanged. He gets progressively older and more irascible. And, of course, as with all programs, he sometimes strikes out.

The nature of guidance

What is guidance? It is difficult to fashion a definition that is both all-inclusive and concise. A high school guidance program encompasses such a range of activities! A grossly untechnical description is that high school guidance attempts to help the student get the most out of his high school experience. I like this definition—partly because I thought of it myself, but also because it is simple. It includes the ideas of educational, social, and psychological growth but puts the emphasis where it belongs—in the high school. All of which is part of my main thesis in this book—that guidance should be academically oriented. Yes, it should be concerned with the total growth of the child, but only within the framework of the school and recognizing the limitations of the guidance process.

A Philosophy of Guidance

Basic to any understanding of guidance and the counselor's job is a philosophy of guidance. It is vitally important that whatever philosophy is adopted by a school be accepted without reservations by the entire counseling staff.

The following is a philosophy created and adopted by four experienced counselors in our school. It may or may not fit your school. I offer it as an example of a scholastically-centered guidance point of view.

"We believe the function of guidance is to assist the student in obtaining the maximum benefit from his high school experience. This very broad statement implies guidance activities that touch every phase of a pupil's development. We feel, however, that our chief concern should be with scholastic problems. Social and psychological problems obviously cannot be ignored, but time and training preclude extensive activity along these lines. Accordingly, our program is intended to be scholastically oriented.

"We believe that, as counselors, our task is to aid the student in making wise decisions and choices that will result in the widest range of post-high school experiences of the highest quality.

"Basic to our *modus operandi* is the conviction that guidance, while a 'soft process,' is not a passive function. We believe in the authoritarian structure of the school and in our responsibility to support this structure.

"We believe in the right of the student for self-determination and, in turn, in his obligation to accept the responsibility for the consequences of his decisions. But we also feel an obligation to influence these decisions in the light of our training and experience.

"In that part of the program that is planned, we feel we should concern ourselves chiefly with choice of school program, adjustment to course requirements, adjustment to the school society, and the choice of post-high school experiences."

The Academically Oriented Guidance Program

I would like to return to the idea of the academically oriented guidance program. This is a program which is planned within the framework of the school and its purposes, concerned with school programs and with all pupils, not just those with personal problems. Its aims will be devoted primarily towards educational goals—not "life adjustment." It will be concerned with such routine functions as careful course selection and planning, evaluation of pupil's interests and abilities, selection of post-high school education and occupation. It will assist the pupil in adjusting to the demands of the classroom and the school society. These activities will constitute the *planned* program.

It is natural that the *planned* program be the sum of many routine procedures—but no less important because they are routine and unspectacular. It could be more important to the future opportunity of a young man to "guide" him into a course in algebra rather than to spend hours in a Rogerian effort to help him accept a new stepmother. I think we would have a better chance to get him to accept the school situation. Of course, if he has a real problem with a stepmother, he may not accept either, and then we're in trouble.

What we are talking about here is again a matter of emphasis. Much as we would like to be all things to all pupils and have the power to solve all their problems, we must realize that even guidance counselors have their limitations. We are deluding ourselves if we think we can mend a broken home, rehabilitate an alcoholic parent, or even motivate the majority of our under-achievers. Yet these are among the very common problems that affect youngsters' achievement and development. We cannot ignore such problems. We have an obligation to help these students in every way possible, and, in many cases, we *can* help—sometimes significantly. But if we try to turn the guidance department into a social agency or psychiatric clinic, we cannot possibly win. We just don't have the resources.

One of the realities of counseling for most of us is the element of time, particularly the lack of it. If the counselor plans to see his 250 to 300 (usually much more, regrettably) counselees a minimum of twice a year, he will have to keep hopping. Assuming a counseling session of at least fifteen minutes, this will amount to between twenty to twenty-five days of full-time counseling—days which just don't exist. A normal counselor's day is a day of interruptions. The phone rings constantly, teachers and parents want to see us, college representatives visit, and we are involved in testing, conferences, special programs, placement, follow-up, and all the other paraphernalia of the guidance office. There is almost no time for the coffee break, let alone a good catharsis. And, of course, many sessions will last longer than fifteen minutes (the unplanned program keeps intruding). Of course, we see many of our students more than twice—particularly seniors.

Under these circumstances, the counselor must choose between those things he *can* do and those things he can only *hope* to do. The choice is clear to me. He will plan a program centered around the school situation, concerned with school problems and with the ultimate fruits of learning. He will be concerned with school adjustment first—with life adjustment second. For the majority of students, this is a legitimate attitude. After all, successful school adjustment *is* successful life adjustment. As I said before, it's all a matter of emphasis.

To my mind, if this planned program were all that a counselor was expected to do, it would certainly justify the counselor's existence.

The role of the counselor

If the counselor is not a psychoanalyst, a professional big brother, or a self-deified do-gooder, what is he?

A high school counselor occupies a unique position in the school organization, outside of the formality of the classroom and apart from the authority of the administration. This does not isolate him from either, however. He is under the authority and supervision of the school principal and has a responsibility both to him and to the faculty to aid in the process of formal education. It *does* place him in a position to approach pupils on an informal "one to one" basis. From this vantage point it is the counselor's job to help the youngster select and carry through a school program that will lead to the best opportunity for a successful post-high school experience. A very important part of this task includes aiding the student to enter a school or job that will result in the maximum self-fulfillment.

Implicit in such a process is decision making on the part of the pupil. It is the counselor's task to present facts and spell out alternatives that will lead to wise choices. In so doing, the counselor may, at the same time, contribute to the social, moral and psychological growth of the child—as do the other agencies of the school, all of which are concerned with "total growth." But he has the time to concentrate on the total picture and he is, or should be, more accessible.

Another way of putting it (to satisfy the psychologists) is that the counselor aids in ego identity and in helping the youngster develop his power to cope with the world and its problems. I hold, however, that he should focus on school problems and work towards the end that the pupil will be comfortable and reasonably successful in his school experience.

Since the counselor is dealing with education, he should be an educator. He should understand the values of liberal arts—much of the high school curriculum is liberal arts on a secondary level—and believe in these values. I feel he has a strong responsibility to identify and interpret these values to his counselees. Today the whole mixed-up mess of marks, parental pressures, and false standards has resulted in confused values in the minds of most students. We should help the pupil to establish healthy and realistic educational values. If *we* don't, who will?

We should help the student to accept and adjust to the demands of an authoritarian situation. This is sometimes difficult in the face of extreme parental permissiveness. I believe that most kids recognize the fact that there is a right and a wrong, although it often gets confused. I'm also convinced that they want the boundaries clearly defined and maintained—both at home and in school. So the counselor, while not actively participating in discipline, is concerned with helping the student develop self-discipline, respect for authority, and respect for self.

This acceptance of authority often results in opportunities to discuss other value formations. We should help our counselees to accept the imperfection of humans, to accept failure, and welcome change as a reality of life. I'm not saying that this is easy, but it is a legitimate function of guidance.

To further identify the role of the counselor and to differentiate between him and other members of the high school family (Remember both teachers and administrators engage in valuable guidance activities every day—sometimes more effectively than we ourselves do!), the following descriptions may help.

The counselor is a repository of facts (or where to find them) about occupations, educational opportunities, community resources, etc.

He is familiar with the curriculum and faculty, and is the one person (with the possible exception of the custodian) who sees the school and its operation in its entirety and with a neutral point of view.

He is well versed in the value and limitations of tests and records because of his training and experience. He is able (hopefully) to form an accurate appraisal of a student's abilities and limitations.

His is an easily accessible shoulder to cry on. Since I added girls to my counselees, I have gone through three gross of Kleenex boxes. Boys usually don't cry—but they sometimes need to spout to someone. Providing this shoulder can be a very significant service—much like the patient bartender who provides a similar opportunity for emotional catharsis to his commuter clients. Whereas I go slow on the martinis, I've often dispensed lemon drops at these times of crisis—an admittedly inferior prescription.

Finally, I believe the counselor should try to encourage the youngster to see himself as a unique individual. In our conformist society, it is our job to help the student establish and develop his individuality—and this within the authoritarian framework of the school. I firmly believe that even the slowest, most limited kid in the school has unlimited potential for giving something of value to the world. Our task is to convince him of this fact—a tough assignment.

The counselor is in an excellent position to evaluate the curriculum and recommend additions and changes. In so doing, he can be a valuable aid to the principal. In our school, for instance, we have recently added a general algebra course, an economics course, and a senior general math review course. In each case, while this was a common venture involving a cooperative faculty and principal, the impetus came from the guidance department, which recognized the need. Counselors can evaluate the effectiveness of college and business preparation through their numerous outside contacts and follow-ups, and make suggestions to teachers that may result in curriculum adjustments. The same is true of much of the routine of the school and some of its policies. This can only be done, however, if there is mutual trust and respect between faculty, administration, and guidance staff.

THE COUNSELOR AND THE TEACHER

The counselor works closely with the classroom teacher. A student who has problems in the classroom is usually referred to the counselor. These problems run the gamut from the under-achiever to the emotionally disturbed child. These cases often end up as part of the *unplanned* program. The counselor supplies the teacher with information about the pupil to assist him in understanding the pupil. This information may consist of test scores, family background, pupil interests, physical disabilities, personality traits, etc. Conversely, the teacher may provide much the same information on certain other students. Ideally, the teacher and counselor work as a team, each complementing the other's work. I can't emphasize strongly enough the importance of this relationship.

THE COUNSELOR AND THE PARENT

The counselor is an advisor to parents as well as to pupils. He acts as liaison between faculty and family.

It is important to keep parents informed. I have found the telephone a more satisfactory instrument than letters. Of course, a face to face visit is even better, and we should not shrink from the prospect of having our privacy invaded during the evenings in cases where both parents work. At our school, we even experimented with evening office hours once or twice a month, but it didn't pay off. We didn't get any business, although others might fare better.

We send out routine information at various times: the usual report cards, mid-term failure notices, a freshman handbook, pupil requests to change courses, information to freshmen on the four-year program at registration time, information on scholarships and procedures for school and college admissions. We hold a parents' night for the purpose of discussing these last two items. It's an informal question and answer period followed by a coffee hour, and has proved to be very effective.

Of course, there is much we should do on a planned basis. However, the phone is always at hand and is usually ringing!

It's been my experience that most parents are genuinely concerned for their children and are usually more in need of guidance themselves, or at least a good sedative. More often than not, they blame themselves for the inadequacies of their children, and many certainly worry too much about them. So another of the counselor's jobs is to reassure distraught mothers and fathers. I'm a great believer in two things: first, that kids usually are in difficulties because of what they are and their particular stage of development rather than because of faulty upbringing (although I'll admit there are plenty of exceptions); second, most of these "problem" kids will usually "make it" in their own time and to a degree that never fails to astonish us all. If there is a common factor in these cases of belated bloomers, it is that they were loved by their parents and knew it. It certainly is not an original idea, but it seems to me that most of our teen-agers' usual problems are solved eventually—often without benefit of guidance (of this we can never be sure) if they have been raised with a modicum of discipline and plenty of parental affection. Mostly they grow up, I guess.

These are all statements unsupported by statistical evidence in our town. But I continually see the tremendous changes wrought by just a few years among our graduates, and I feel better about them. These are years of rapid change and we see the youngsters at their absolute worst! One graying mother put it aptly when she wished she could "bury them at 13 and dig them up when they were 18." It is well to keep in mind, and to remind parents, that we evaluate high school kids on a very limited basis—primarily on their scholastic success. Unfortunately, many of the more important traits that make for a worthwhile life are largely ignored. We don't give marks for honesty and integrity, a concern for others, the ability to get along with others, etc. But these are obviously more valuable than the ability to crack an "A" in Algebra.

We must help parents weather the stormy, difficult teen-age years. And don't expect them to be realistic about their children. I'm not, and I should know better! Too bad they haven't invented a patience pill to go along with the other one.

Summary

By way of summary of the guidance counselor's role, I am including the following job description which attempts to put the program in capsule form.

For the pupil:

1. To assist the pupil in realistic self-appraisal.
2. To encourage the choice and successful completion of a scholastic program that is consistent with the pupil's abilities and that will lead to the widest possible choice of post-high school opportunities.
3. To assist the pupil in adjusting to the scholastic, social and personal demands of his school life.
4. To assist the pupil in developing realistic vocational aims.
5. To encourage every pupil to enter some sort of post-high school training.
6. To assist in job placement.

For the faculty:

1. To aid teachers by providing those guidance services that make their efforts more effective.

For the administration:

1. To assist in evaluating the overall educational program and to recommend changes and additions to the school curriculum.

For the parents:

1. To inform parents of their children's progress, limitations, and abilities as evidenced in the school.
2. To aid parents in the post-high school planning.
3. To help parents understand their children and their needs.

This chapter has tried to describe the concepts of guidance and the role of the counselor as I see them. That my view is shared by the majority of veteran counselors in our area may or may not be significant. However, if experience is the best teacher, then the conclusions described above are inevitable. As counselors, we must decide whether we are going to accept the original concept of guidance as an adjunct to the process of formal education or take off into the wild blue yonder on a giddy, exciting psychological binge. I'm afraid the latter approach, while tempting to the idealistic newcomer to guidance, is bound to fail if attempted within the average high school by the average counselor.

2

The Counselor
at Work

A Day in the Salt Mines

This chapter will deal with the counselor and his primary function—counseling. We'll examine such phases as gaining rapport, counseling techniques, the planned program and means of evaluating it. I have included a brief peek at the counselor during a typical day which I hope my principal will read—it may convince him that we counselors really work. I have also added a few gentle words of advice which I hope will be helpful to the novice.

The raw material

The high school years are years of rapid development and change. During these four years a child becomes an adult—or nearly so (even the most sophisticated senior still has a lot of little boy left in him). The social and physiological changes involved result in a variety of problems and pressures. All this is well known, but it might be well to review the characteristics of our young clients.

If there are such things as typical adolescents, they usually can be recognized by these hallmarks:

They are idealistic, fiercely loyal champions of the underdog. They are dreamers and completely unrealistic. They are intensely concerned with self. As a result they are selfish, thoughtless and often obnoxious—particularly at home. They are overly sensitive and self-conscious. They are gregarious—or want to be. They are unsure of themselves and hide this from the adult world and from each other in many ways.

Friendships with others their own age are very important. They give them a feeling of security—of belonging. Since they usually distrust their capacity to enter the adult world, they form a special society closed off from adults in many ways. Don't try to enter it without being invited! As a result, communication between parents and progeny is often difficult, if not nonexistent.

They are rebellious, resisting authority and searching for greater freedom. At the same time, they need and want the security of authority, of having the bounds firmly established and enforced. They want to have their cake and eat it too!

They wear their hair too long or their skirts too short. They are too loud or too shy. They are contradictory, moody, demanding and difficult. And with it all, they are among the most charming of God's creatures.

The "one-to-one" relationship

Long ago we came to the realization that all individuals are unique—different from each other, different from their parents, and with tremendous variation in basic abilities and talents. The general high school will house students from widely varying backgrounds and socio-economic levels. We group them together in a classroom with some attempt to sort them by reason of ability and interest. But it is primarily in the counseling process that the pupil is treated as an individual, where the focus is solely on him and his ideas, his dreams, and his problems. The strength of any guidance program lies in the "one-to-one" relationship between counselor and pupil. If this relationship is a poor one, if the pupil cannot "relate" successfully to his counselor, then no amount of organization and programming can keep the guidance program from failure. This is one reason why, if I were hiring counselors,

I'd concentrate on personal traits rather than on the degree of graduate training. Of course, no counselor can hope to gain rapport with all his pupils, but if he is sincerely interested in them, the vast majority will respond in kind.

This private and close relationship can be found in many other places in the school, of course. As I have mentioned before, many teachers enjoy this kind of trust. These people can be of valuable assistance to the youngster and help in transferring some of this feeling to the counselor. But because of the counselor's unique position in the school, because of his ability to view the entire scene, and because he has the time and is available, he has the best chance to build up a good pupil relationship. This rapport is essential for individual counseling, which is the core of the guidance program.

Building rapport

I don't know whether a conscious effort to build trust and acceptance by the pupil can pay off. However, in thinking about this, several ideas come to mind.

First, it is necessary that the counselor be *available*. Most schools have relieved the counselor from lunch duty, detention, etc. To this end, in addition, the counselor should try to keep himself unencumbered by paper work, reports, and any activity that takes him away from the pupils while they are in school. Paper work should be done after school hours, leaving the maximum amount of time during the school day free for counseling. Sometimes, the counselor must make a choice. I'm afraid the records in our school are not in the best condition at this writing. But, lacking adequate clerical help, we have simply made the decision to concentrate on counseling to the detriment of other phases of guidance. This, of course, results in a weakness in our program, but I'd rather it be in the area of record keeping than in that of counseling.

I might say a word about the counseling environment. There should be at least the illusion of privacy. Our offices are tiny cubicles, but they are enclosed, reasonably soundproof, and provide the needed isolation. My own office is cluttered, disorganized and informal, but it has a comfortable, "lived-in" feeling. I can't imagine anyone feeling an atmosphere of austerity or impersonality when entering. I might add that I have two abstract paintings on the wall which I did myself. They're there partly to build up my own ego, and partly because, although lacking in artistic merit, they are colorful. I often start a session by asking the youngster which one he likes better (sort of a Jackson Pollack ink-blot test), and that leads to a variety of conversation— much of it not particularly kind to my artistic self-image. I'm not seriously proposing that counselors should take a course in oil painting, of course, but I wish to emphasize that the atmosphere of the counseling room be informal, warm and "comfortable."

If the counselor should be readily available, it's also necessary that the students be equally available. We usually see students outside of classroom time, for obvious reasons. Study halls are the best time, as well as before and after school. Our administration, however, has authorized us to take pupils from classes when necessary—a privilege that must not be overworked. In other words, it is necessary that the administration provide time during the school day when pupils can visit the guidance office. Incidentally, youngsters will take advantage of this, if possible, and we use a system of passes to discourage unauthorized or unnecessary visits. The pupils can drop in between classes and ask us to take them out of their study halls for counseling. This all may seem like "much ado about nothing," but I do know of schools with guidance programs where the kids are practically unavailable during the school day.

Building rapport is a long process and is usually the result of many encounters between counselor and client. For this reason we schedule routine interviews for the freshmen (or sophomores in a 3-3 junior high-senior high system) as often as we can to get acquainted. I often drop into homerooms before school on any pretext to stop and chat with some of these strangers. A word in the corridors or just a greeting—anything to acknowledge recognition—does much to lay the groundwork for eventual acceptance.

I believe a counselor should take part in some extracurricular activity as time permits—attend athletic events, band concerts, and, heaven forbid, school dances. Been to a high school dance lately? Fantastic! I can't escape the conviction that young people today are born with thickened eardrums. And they are all double-jointed in extraordinary places.

Interest in the youngster as evidenced by the simplest act may lead to a beginning of acceptance. I have more than once picked up a rather unresponsive counselee and have given him a ride home after school. Our whole relationship changed after that (for the better, I hasten to add). I've taken some of these boys hunting or fishing. Last year I had a visit from a young girl caught in a very unfortunate home situation. I couldn't solve her problem. But I could and did let her cry, get it off her chest, and afterwards we took a short ride so she could have a cigarette and relax. My reward came this year when, after she was accepted by a teacher's college, she came in after the senior assembly to thank her "other father." My point is that any display of genuine interest pays off—and it doesn't take much to make a difference.

It is hard to evaluate the effect of counseling, but usually one or two pupils stand out in your mind as cases in which you played a significant role, and these are great morale builders. I remember Jack from years ago. He was an intelligent, sensitive, immature boy brought up by an "old country" mother. He was the typical under-achiever—unsure, slightly rebellious, the "class clown," and very conscious of his appearance and acceptance by his group. A rather handsome boy, he had a severe case of acne and, quite naturally, was overly sensitive about it. During a ball game he fell and slashed his face badly; the wound was infected and he was hospitalized. I visited him to bring in homework assignments, and in the course of conversation he broke down and insisted he was not coming back to school because of the disfigurement of his face. We talked this out, arranged through the school nurse for plastic surgery, and he eventually returned to school, an act of extreme courage on his part. He worked hard during his senior year, and we arranged for a scholarship at a good prep school. During this post-graduate year, Jack found himself, discovered reading, did well scholastically and finally ended up with an engineering degree from our State University where he paid most of his expenses by part-time and summer jobs.

I'm not sure of the psychology behind this transformation, but I'm sure of one thing: if I hadn't visited him in the hospital, Jack might never have finished high school—much less college. So a small act sometimes pays off in big dividends. And, of course, there were many other understanding people who played a very important part in the metamorphosis.

GETTING ACQUAINTED

It is obvious that the counselor should keep the same counselees during their stay in high school. It's impossible to get to know them in one year. We recently changed to a 3-3 system (which counselors and teachers alike abhor), and I can see the difference in how well I know my seniors. That extra year makes a tremendous difference. We can still operate effectively, but how we wish we had those students as freshmen!

There are several ways in which one can get a picture of the individual, his background, and interests. One is a questionnaire which includes such items as home situation, interests, hobbies and plans. This, coupled with an autobiography—possibly done in English classes—sometimes can be enlightening. But it won't reveal how the youngster feels about himself, his family, or his school. And don't include questions involving emotions or attitudes, because the answers you get will not usually be accurate. After all, *I* wouldn't tell a total stranger that I hated my father. I probably wouldn't admit it to myself. For this reason, I hold all questionnaires that purport to identify problem areas of this sort in deep distrust. Kids are not so insensible that they cannot see the purpose behind such devices and, quite naturally, feel an invasion of privacy—something which counselors should respect with maximum prudence.

This matter of confidentialness and respect for privacy is at the base of any trust enjoyed by a counselor. I am careful, first of all, to avoid probing into personal matters unless the youngster brings them up himself. I may offer my help if I feel something is bothering him, but I don't force the issue. When a student spills out a story involving a home situation which seems to warrant follow-up, I ask permission of the student to talk with the parents. Quite often he may say no—feeling it might make matters worse. This sometimes leaves one in an awkward position, but there have been few cases when I did not acquiesce to the pupil's wishes. Often we can do more harm by meddling. Then, too, sometimes youngsters tend to color or exaggerate a situation out of proportion to the actual case. And sometimes, being human, they lie!

I can remember two recent instances of reported pregnancies that were pure fabrication on the part of the youngsters. They didn't "confess" to me, but leaked the "news" to their friends. Don't ask me why—maybe an attempt to gain attention and status. High school pregnancies do get a lot of attention even in our sophisticated society. I can even document a case of purported incest which was blithely chronicled by the supposed victim to one of our young and unsophisticated teachers. That shook me up! Fortunately, it too turned out to be inaccurate. Of course, all of these cases reflected symptoms of emotional disturbance, but all these kids are now happily married and apparently stable individuals. The lesson here is: Although these things can happen— and as a matter of fact, have happened—proceed with caution. And lean over backwards to respect a youngster's privacy.

TECHNIQUES OR INVOLVEMENT?

A sizable amount of guidance literature and field training is concerned with counseling techniques. Whether to be nondirective or directive, the use and analysis of tape recordings, and the use of group therapy and psychodramas are all the subject of extensive inquiry and research. I can't get too excited by these techniques, although one always learns something useful from them. I have the strong conviction that if a counselor is truly involved with his counselee and has built up a good relationship, he doesn't need to use techniques—just understanding and common sense. In our school I have found, along with my colleagues, that if a youngster has a problem, he will usually tell you about it if you ask him. It's as simple as that. If he isn't ready to talk about it, you couldn't help him anyway. Our problem is not to identify sources of maladjustment and difficulty, but to do something about it when we find out the trouble. Therefore, I don't believe one should be too concerned with counseling techniques. Personal involvement, a sincere interest and respect for the individual, will usually be all the techniques you need. Most of us do not have time to be purely nondirective. While I respect the theory behind the approach (read *Dibs* [1]—an absorbing drama of a disturbed child), this belongs in the clinical psychologist's book of tricks. A counselor cannot passively sit back and elicit a detailed report of a problem from the counselee with a series of grunts, assents, and long periods of silence. Time does not permit this. We must control the situation more than that. If the problem is so deep-seated that such a technique is necessary, it may be a case for referral. This is a dangerous generality to make since, usually, an unwillingness to talk is merely an indication of lack of rapport rather than a deep-seated emotional problem. Of course, there will be other evidence throughout the school in those cases of serious emotional difficulties.

GUIDANCE OR DIRECTION?

There is always the danger that a counselor can be too directive and take the initiative away from his counselee. We should listen more and talk less. We should be careful not to promote our own attitudes or ideas to the exclusion of the youngster's. We can't decide for him. Our job is to describe possible courses of action and alternatives. By the same token, if our experience makes us feel strongly that a certain course of action is best, there's nothing wrong in saying so, providing we leave the youngster with the feeling that we will respect and accept whatever course he decides upon. To do less is to give up a responsibility to guide, and we will just end up as professional fence-sitters. There is admittedly a fine line between guiding and directing, but common sense should point the way. It's fine to say that kids should be allowed to make mistakes and thereby learn. But in the case of a bright pupil who is unwilling to take a language yet wants eventually to attend a liberal arts college (and who has the ability to do so), the counselor, who knows that the language is a requirement at most colleges, is justified in forceful remonstrance. In most such cases, once the facts are pointed out to family and pupil, the point is successfully made. I call this directive guidance, but anything else would be ridiculous. I grant that

---

[1] Virginia M. Axline, *Dibs: In Search of Self* (Boston, Mass.: Houghton Mifflin Co., 1964).

this is a simple example, but it is intended merely as an illustration of the kinds of routine decisions faced all the time by pupils—decisions where the counselor's experience and knowledge should be used to full advantage.

A four-year counseling plan

There are many decisions that have to be made at certain times in the high school career of the pupil, beginning with the choice of curriculum and culminating in the choice of post-high school activity. Some of these such as occupational or school choice involve continuing activity. These are the items of the planned program which we have discussed.

We usually begin the year by seeing each of our new counselees as soon as possible, just to say hello, introduce ourselves, and check the pupil's program for errors and any signs of early scholastic difficulties. We next turn to the seniors, particularly those that are going on to school. And, during a series of interviews with each individual, we attempt to get all school applications completed before Christmas. This usually strings out well into March for some of them, however, due to indecision, change of plans and the like. In our school, only about 30 per cent of each class goes directly into a four-year school, but another 35 per cent goes on to some sort of school. Consequently, this keeps us busy during most of the fall. January gives us a chance to see our freshmen again because we are getting ready for course registration in March for the following year. We go over the four-year plan very carefully at that time in the light of their record to date and make any adjustments necessary. We also see the sophomores and juniors to check their programs. This is a busy time because we have to see ¾ of our counselees in a little over two short months. Spring is a period for juniors. We start talking more specifically about schools, jobs, or the service so that by fall they have some idea as to the direction they will take. We try to work in a final check with the freshmen and sophomores on their courses by the end of the year. Spring is also a period of job placement for seniors and last minute decisions involving work, school or the service. Of course, other activities are carried on concurrently. If one has a group guidance program, some of the above can be done in guidance classes, but the timing would be about the same. (More on the possibilities of group guidance classes later.) Worked into this schedule will be a testing program. We also see each student who receives a warning of failure at midterm or a failure at the end of a term. I question whether we help many of these pupils much, but we are sometimes able to make certain adjustments and we certainly get to know some of them very well indeed! I think it pays off in the long run in terms of understanding and rapport.

We have a very flexible curriculum and spend much of our time in making course adjustments for individuals who are in scholastic difficulties for one reason or another. This activity accelerates after each marking period, of course.

The following is a suggested four-year counseling schedule, exclusive of guidance classes and pared to the bone for the sake of simplicity.

Fall: *Freshman orientation interviews.
        *School/occupational planning for seniors.
        PSAT tests in Oct. for juniors.
        *Testing in early Nov. for sophomores (reading and scholastic aptitude).

Winter: *Course planning for freshmen, sophomores, and juniors.
        Occupational aptitude testing for certain selected seniors.
        Continuing school and occupational planning for certain seniors.
        *Interpretation of sophomore tests.
        *Registration for underclassmen.

Spring: *School and occupational planning for juniors.
        National Merit test for certain juniors.
        *Final check on next year's courses with freshmen, sophomores and juniors.
        Job placement for seniors.

  * Indicates an activity involving every pupil in the class.

A quick check will suggest that the sophomores are the neglected class in terms of time spent. However, we do see those individuals needing help with scholastic and personal problems throughout the year, and the rest seem able to struggle on without our assistance.

It is also obvious that many of the interviews will necessarily be brief. It is possible to combine items—test interpretation and course planning for sophomores, for instance.

It also becomes obvious that, if we are to do any kind of job with the planned program, a counselor pupil ratio greater than 1/300 is unrealistic. However, in cases where the ratio is less favorable and one has to cut down on activities, my advice is to concentrate on the four-year pupil program plan at the one end and post-high school planning at the other. These are the two most important pupil decisions and the ones where the counselor's knowledge and experience is most needed.

Some do's and don't's in counseling

The following suggestions are a summary of the opinions of several experienced counselors in our area. Nobody can avoid making mistakes, and periodic soul searching and reassessment is necessary to keep one's perspective.

1. *Don't talk too much.* Do listen. It's easy to jump to the wrong conclusion. First, get the whole story. Then make suggestions.

2. *Don't scold.* Do take a positive approach. We should not stand in judgment of a youngster. For instance, it does no good to bawl a pupil out for not doing as well as you know he can. He is already acutely aware of his deficiencies. His parents have doubtless blasted him, and it serves little purpose for the counselor to join in the stoning. It's almost an irresistible temptation to say the obvious thing. I catch myself doing it all the time. You know: "John, you can do better than this. . . ." Try to suggest a positive approach. Show the youngster ways he can help himself and ways that he can get help from others. Keep faith in him in the hope that he will retain faith in himself. In the case of a pupil who pulls a stupid trick in class or study hall, I can't help but call him a "knot-head," but this is a little different. He knows he's a knot-head and he knows I know it. But he also knows that—while I meant it—I still have respect for him as an individual. My intent is not to tear him down. My approach to one of my newer counselees would be somewhat more restrained.

I guess my point here is that we don't take advantage of weaknesses, but we don't condone foolishness either.

3. *Don't use your job to build up your ego.* It's too easy to say that "I got that boy into Harvard," forgetting that the boy got *himself* into Harvard by *his* hard work, and *his* "Board" scores and *his* contributions to school life. With this kind of thinking, it's too easy to fall into the trap of evaluating our own success by the success of our youngsters. This is putting the cart before the horse. The everyday work we do with those lesser lights of the school may not have as spectacular results as our National Merit winner, but the effort can be more significant and more heart-warming.

4. *Have patience!* As counselors we inhabit an uneasy never-never land between teachers, administrators and parents. Everybody is eager to take a whack at the counselor. He is the educator's fall guy and a tempting target. Don't fight it! Accept it. Glory in it. Bite the bullet and don't let them get you down! My own rule for dealing with grown-ups is: Never expect them to act reasonably. Of course, I'm exaggerating slightly. But it isn't usually the kids who give us trouble. It's the grown-ups. It takes much tact, diplomacy and many a honeyed word to get the job done. And then don't expect any thanks. The parent or pupil who actually expresses gratitude appears about 1 in 100 on the average. Of course, the youngsters say it in other ways, such as coming back after they've graduated, by hanging around the office, or merely by smiling at you when you see them in the corridor.

5. *Cultivate a sense of humor* or, maybe more to the point, a sense of good humor. Kids respond to a smile. They can be cajoled with kidding easier than they can be forced by bombast. Help them to take their troubles, if not lightly, at least with a sense of proportion and balance.

6. *Don't talk down to students.* Respect them and their problems no matter how ridiculous they seem. Treat every youngster as if he were your only client.

7. *Be scrupulously honest.* Never go behind a pupil's back. Respect confidences. At the same time, one doesn't need to be brutal about it. We should always build up the youngster. If I am interpreting a low I.Q. score to a student, I never say he is at the bottom of the class. Instead I say that he is at the lower end of

the average range. I think that is harmless double-talk. (After all, the mere fact that he has reached high school would put him in the broad range of average abilities in most places.) However, we can't expect to help a youngster accept his limitations unless he knows what they are—as nearly as we can judge, at least, with the admittedly imperfect instruments at hand.

8. *Respect the classroom teacher.* Avoid interrupting his work. Help the learning process. That's why the kids are in school!

9. *Keep parents informed.* In fact, keep all lines of communication open—to parents, to teachers, to administrators and to the community. Ignorance of the facts breeds problems.

Evaluation of the counseling program

Like clergymen, we can never evaluate accurately the effectiveness of our efforts. We deal largely in intangibles. However, there are a few rough measures of our success.

As far as the more routine functions of job and school placement are concerned—and these are primary aims of the program—the yearly follow-up should indicate something to us. The counselor should have a fairly good idea of the intellectual and cultural make-up of his student body. He knows, for instance, that a certain percentage have high I.Q.'s of 115 and above. Generally speaking, these are the students that should be going on to college. Are these pupils electing the college course and later entering college? If not, why not? There may be factors working against you—socio-economic backgrounds, isolation from centers of education, etc. But the counselor should at least be aware of them.

Equally important, how many of the others are going on to some kind of school? Does the history of the last five classes show a steady increase in both areas? These are questions which may lead to some relevant conclusions.

The same yardstick may be applied to pupils going on to work. Just how good is the placement service? What kind of jobs are they getting? Is there more the guidance program can do to ensure maximum opportunity?

I would not attempt to evaluate a program by these criteria without looking into the whole picture and discovering the limitations of the community and the character of the student body. An affluent community peopled by professional men and successful businessmen will send as much as 95 per cent of their children to college. We send about 40 per cent. But the cultural and intellectual levels of the two student bodies are quite different. I don't pretend to claim that the percentage of placement is a reflection of a school's merit (although many parents would try to claim this). It is only one area of evaluation.

Another measure is the number of drop-outs per year. The same community characteristics apply here. But the counselor should investigate these matters and question school policies and guidance procedures if he cannot find reasonable answers.

A third and rather limited approach is the academic inventory as proposed by Dr. Conant in his treatise on the American High School. In this, one selects all those seniors of the past graduating class who scored in the top 15 per cent in the I.Q. tests or who received an "A" in elementary algebra. Their four-year school record is plotted on a card and then compared to the ideal program for these gifted children. Such a program would include four years each of English, social studies, mathematics, science and language. Obviously, this group could be expected to fare well scholastically and enter college. Few students in our school completely satisfy this ideal—for numerous reasons. But the point is that it raises questions and sometimes is quite surprising in what it reveals. I have found that often the top quarter of the class did as well as the top 15 per cent. Possessing a high I.Q. does not automatically bequeath the pupil with the will or ability to use it. But, as a rough measure of both scheduling effectiveness, quality of teaching, counseling, and college placement, the academic inventory is a useful tool. It leads to self-questioning and re-examination of guidance procedures and is valuable if only for that reason. If a high percentage of the gifted in your school do not take a program paralleling this, or do not successfully carry it through to college, let's find out why not.

Finally, and perhaps the most convincing evidence that the guidance program is functioning effectively is the number of pupils who seek your help voluntarily, both those enrolled currently, as well as those that have been out for a year or more. These are the proof that you are operating effectively.

A day in the life of a counselor

7:45 Arrive at school. Greeted by four students wishing passes for interviews during their study periods. Issue passes. Next a five-minute conversation with Dorothy, deep in a dilemma, since she has been asked to the prom by two boys, both of whom she wants to date. Stall and beat a hasty retreat to the principal's office. Bell rings. Return to guidance office.

8:05 Phone rings. Disturbed mother inquiring about a failure notice in algebra received by son. Make note to see teacher and boy.

8:07 Phone rings. Trustee of scholarship fund calls to arrange meeting of directors and guidance counselors.

8:10 Visit senior homerooms to check on latest plans of seniors not going on to school. Schedule two interviews. Visit to men teachers' room. Check with Problems of Democracy teacher on two senior boys on danger list. Return to office.

8:30 Call down one of the Prob. of Democ. boys. Arrange for study hall in library for two weeks. Spend 30 seconds wondering why seniors have to be led by the hand like babies. Bell rings.

8:45 Consult with boy failing algebra. Seems he is one of those kids who freezes on tests. Possible explanation of disappointing junior year. (Why didn't I find this out earlier!) Arrange for special sessions with teacher on test days.

9:30 Coffee break for counselors in principal's office. Discussion of credit for summer make-up work in cases of failure in required courses. Discussion of proposed new course in architectural drafting. Brief exchange of information involving one counselor's ulcer, another's precocious six-year old, and my brilliant eight-year old boy. Nobody listens to me.

10:00 Back to the office. Read mail. Throw away most and arrange rest for circulation to counselors. Discover that at least four good midwestern schools still have room for qualified applicants. Bell rings.

10:15 Call in senior girl who has been refused admission at college of first choice and who doesn't want to go locally. Suggest one of the midwestern colleges and then introduce the idea of using one of the college placement services. She buys this and exits with application. (She later receives 20 offers of admission from good schools.)

10:45 Interviews with three juniors on schools. Two did not take May college boards. Give them applications for July exams. Spend 30 seconds wondering to myself why juniors have to be led by the hand like babies. They certainly should have known— what with the assembly and information sheet. Oh well!

11:45 See student who wishes to change course for next year. Long discussion involving school plans and admission requirements. Call student's home for clarification. Student exits, apparently accepting the inevitable, but with reservations. (Student later fails the course. Strike one!)

12:15 Lunch at local sandwich shop. Spirited discussion of Vietnam situation with two truck drivers and the local judge. I agree with truck drivers. Reports on trout fishing from several regulars whose veracity is immediately put in doubt.

1:00 Back to office. See two more juniors about post-high school plans. Why does every girl want to be a hairdresser? In our town, there must be a hairdresser for every four women. Arrange for a representative of hairdressing school to come in to talk with those interested.

1:45 Session with one of the senior boys—a teacher referral. John feels lost. He doesn't know what he is interested in, distrusts his abilities, questions whether he can fit into the adult world. Arrange for G.A.T.B. (General Aptitude Test Battery) at local state division of employment security. Discuss possible P.G. course. Make mental note to follow up this one soon. He seems really despondent. This isn't the first of such interviews, incidentally. How to build up his feeling of adequacy, of personal worth?

2:20 Quick check with other senior boy failing Prob. of Democ. Seems aware of situation and apparently is doing all he can. Nothing I can do here.

2:30 Bell rings. School's out. Sounds of powerful engines revving in the parking lot. Squeals, laughter, horns, then comparative quiet. Write out 2 recommendations for students applying late to schools. Think about John for 10 minutes. Write letters to parents of boys failing Prob. of Democ. outlining situation and pointing out that they might not graduate. (Expect two calls in two days.) Think about John for 5 minutes.

3:15 Meeting with guidance and administrative personnel as part of current curriculum study and evaluation.

4:30 Leave for home. Maybe I'll have time for a fishing trip to the middle branch after supper. Those guys at lunch might have been telling the truth.

This is a representative day, mostly routine, mostly undramatic —only one serious problem of a personal nature, and this was a tough one. Actually, John's case turned out to be serious enough to warrant referral. I do not know at this writing what the outcome will be.

Summary

This chapter has been concerned with the important counselor-client relationship and has charted a course based on a scholastic approach to the planned program. Other chapters will deal with the unplanned problems that make the job less routine and often frustrating. But it is in the planned program that we *can* do something tangible, something helpful, something of value for *every* pupil.

3

Developing the
Testing Program

Genius or Over-Achiever

The purpose of testing is to find out something you don't already know. In guidance, we also are looking for corroborative evidence of things we suspect to be true. Why test at all? Because we're continually evaluating our young clients and because we've already seen that the academic record, although the most valid predictor of scholastic success, is often misleading. There are many factors that prevent a child from achieving up to capacity, so another ability measure is useful. Since we use tests that are standardized on a national or regional basis, we have a method of comparing our students with others.

Types of group tests

Because of the limitations of time, group tests are the commonly used tools of evaluation employed by high schools. There are several general categories of standardized tests found in high school use.

1. Scholastic Aptitude (Intelligence) Tests

These are tests that attempt to measure basic abilities commonly used in school. They test the student's capacity to learn. They are all multi-factor tests. Some produce a single score—a kind of average—while others produce a separate score for each factor tested. As to the single score tests, they may be standardized on an age level scale, that is, equated with the national average at a particular age. In this case they are commonly expressed as an Intelligence Quotient. I.Q. $= \dfrac{\text{test age}}{\text{actual age.}}$ A quotient of one is expressed as one hundred, 1.10 as 110, etc. The average is usually around 100+ for any test. A score of 115 or better is indicative of a bright student; less than 90 usually indicates a slow student. This is oversimplification, of course, but I do not intend to get involved in the subject of psychometrics at this writing, or any other for that matter. Most tests are also expressed as a percentile. Thus an I.Q. of 100 would correspond to the 50th percentile. This correlation varies considerably among tests at their more extreme ranges. For example, in one test an I.Q. of 115 would lie in the 75th percentile—on another it might correspond to the 80th percentile. It depends on the particular standardization. This is one reason why I prefer the percentile score. A percentile of 85 means the same for any test; that is, 85 per cent of the group tested scored lower. The I.Q. score needs far more interpretation. Incidentally, we report both scores to colleges and schools. Examples of this type of test are the California Test of Mental Maturity and the Otis Test of Mental Abilities. The former produces three I.Q. scores—verbal, non-verbal and total.

The second form of Scholastic Ability Test is the one which produces several scores—usually expressed in percentiles—in a number of areas: verbal, numerical, abstract reasoning, space relations, mechanical and the like. These tests have obvious advantages providing the counselor does not fall into the trap of using them to *limit* course selection unduly. The Differential Aptitude Test (D.A.T.) is an example.

Although we use all these tests in our system, I prefer the single score test. This is not because it's better but because I've become used to it, its characteristics and limitations. I don't pretend that any one test is better than the other. They are all useful and they are all imperfect.

2. SPECIAL APTITUDE TESTS

These are tests that test special abilities such as reading, one of the most useful in the group. No skill is as important to scholastic success as this. The Coöperative and Iowa Reading Tests are well-known examples. Other kinds of aptitude tests include tests of space relations, mechanical aptitude, language aptitude and so on ad infinitum. All of these can be useful at times with certain individuals. If you included them all in a battery, you'd spend an inordinate amount of time in testing. However, a Guidance Department can stock a small number of these tests to be given to individuals as the occasion arises.

3. TESTS OF INTERESTS, ATTITUDES, PERSONALITY AND ADJUSTMENT INVENTORIES

The Occupational Inventory is popular in many schools and is used in connection with occupational choice. This can be moderately useful if one doesn't expect too much of it. These are multiple choice tests where the student is asked to indicate a preference or dislike for a certain type of task characteristic of a particular job field. For example:

B1 "Would you rather milk cows and plant corn?" (Natural field jobs concerning plants and animals)

or

C2 "Would you rather change tires and grease cars?" (Mechanical field)

The pattern of responses to a number of questions in each job field is supposed to indicate occupational interest.

These inventories can be useful in initiating a discussion of occupational choice—sometimes they reflect real and permanent interests. But I'd hate to plan my career on the basis of one of these inventories taken in my sophomore year. I would have ended up as a combination Forester, Artist, and Harem Keeper. The trouble is that the test does nothing to inform a youngster about the world of work or himself. It just asks the question,

"What job would you pick if you had to choose now?" in a round-about way and elicits answers based on incomplete knowledge.

Some *attitude* and *personality tests* purport to spot the potential problem child. You can use them if you want to—I don't. In any case, pupils should not be *forced* to take them. This prying into the secret thoughts and weaknesses of pupils by a mechanical tool is a transparent device for most youngsters, and I think they resent it. Under ideal circumstances, with mutual consent and understanding, the tests could be helpful. I prefer to rely on a good relationship with the pupil and let him come to me. I don't mean to sound smug; I merely think this is the best way in the long run. Also, we have enough troubles without looking for more. (I'm being facetious—I think.)

I have found a limited use in the kind of personality tests related to job choices. See Chapter 8.

4. GENERAL APTITUDE BATTERIES

These, like the D.A.T., present percentile scores in a number of areas but are not necessarily aimed at the school child. They stress abilities used in occupations and often include performance tests such as finger dexterity and eye-hand coordination. They are commonly used in job placement. The General Aptitude Test Battery (G.A.T.B.) of the U.S. Department of Employment is an example. We have this administered to certain selected seniors each year. Such tests are difficult to administer and take much time.

Individual tests

All schools should have the facilities for and personnel capable of administering individual intelligence tests. These too are time consuming and require skilled, experienced testers but almost invariably produce more accurate (and usually higher) scores. The Stanford-Binet is the classic example. The Wechsler (W.A.I.S. and W.I.S.C.) tests are very popular and less verbal in content. We use the group tests as screening devices and occasionally retest with the individual test in cases where there is doubt about the accuracy of the group test score—as in the case of a very low score or an emotionally disturbed child. Usually we retest with a different form of the same group test, for reasons of time. This seems to accomplish its purpose in most cases.

The purpose and use of standardized tests

When a student enters high school, he is faced with the decision of course selection. The counselor, in aiding the student to choose wisely, must be able to evaluate the youngster's potential as accurately as possible. At that time in our school system, for example, the pupil's permanent record will show several achievement tests taken over the years which indicate his mastery of the tools of learning—reading, the mechanics of English and arithmetic, etc. In addition there will be two Scholastic Aptitute Test results from earlier years and one (the D.A.T.) from junior high. From this and the pupil's academic record, the counselor must estimate the youngster's true ability. On the basis of this evaluation, he helps his counselee outline his plan of studies for high school.

One might think this would be enough testing, but we give a battery in the sophomore year. This consists of an I.Q. test, a Reading Comprehension test and an Occupational Interest Inventory. Our reasons are several. First of all, this is a period of rapid change and development and we are continually turning up a surprisingly high score on some youngster whose previous record and test scores showed mediocre ability. Low scores are subject to doubt, but high scores are usually accurate. You can't get a high score by accident. So this opens up some possibilities and gives us a chance to "schedule up." We're always finding the poor reader who may have been average in grade school, but who has since lost ground. Then we always have several questionable kids whose immaturity or lack of motivation makes it difficult to assess their real ability. Finally, it is well to have several test scores in order to get the most accurate evaluation.

We use this information in scheduling and in predicting scholastic success in college and various other levels of post-high school education, as well as success in different levels of occupations. In general, this predictive function of tests is their main purpose and value in schools. Nobody any longer claims that an I.Q. derived from any test—group or individual—is in itself a true measure of intelligence. Motivation, cultural background, emotional stress all combine to distort the picture. Add to this the fact that the tests themselves are inadequate and incomplete. But, coupled with the record of classroom performance, they are useful. We would be hampered without them, despite their limitations.

Here are some illustrations involving the use of test results. Let's consider the case of Bill, a sophomore in the college course. We are planning the junior year program prior to registration. His record to date:

9th Grade		10th Grade	
Eng. 1C	D	Eng. 2C	D
Geog.	C	Hist. 2C	D
Alg. 1C	E	Alg. 1 (repeat)	C
Gen. Sci.	C	Bio.	C
Latin 1	E	Latin 1 (repeat)	D
Phys. Ed.	B	Phys. Ed.	C

D.A.T. (9th Grade): Verbal 55%tile
Numerical 60%tile
Abstract Reasoning 45%tile

Otis (10th Grade): I.Q. 105

Read Comp: 55%tile

In this case the test scores obviously corroborate what we already suspected. He is over his head as far as the college course is concerned. So after discussion with the parents, we changed to the business course, which we probably should have done the year before. However, we decided to let Bill have a go at Geometry. It's always worth the risk.

Consider Gail, who is at the same point in her sophomore year. She is enrolled in the business course.

9th Grade		10th Grade	
Eng. 1G	B	Eng. 2G	A
Geog.	C	Hist. 2G	B
Gen. Math	A	Bookkeeping	B
Gen. Sci.	B	Bio.	C
Bus. Trng.	A	Typing 1	B
Phys. Ed.	C	Phys. Ed.	B

D.A.T. Verbal: 50%tile
Numerical: 65%tile
Abstract Reasoning: 55%tile

But the Otis Test in the fall of her sophomore year showed an I.Q. of 115. This, coupled with her academic success, prompted me to suggest a change to college English and history and the inclusion of two years of college math and chemistry in her junior and senior years. Would I have suggested this if her tenth grade test had been lower? Probably—in part, at least.

Take the case of Michael, who is making a decision about next year's schedule. He has not fared well.

9th Grade		10th Grade	
Eng. 1C	C	Eng. 2C	D
Geog.	C	Hist. 2C	D
Alg. 1C	C	Geom.	D
Bio.	D	French 2	E
French 1	D	Typing 1	D
Phys. Ed.	C	Phys. Ed.	C

D.A.T. *Verbal:* 90%tile
Numerical: 85%tile
Abstract Reasoning: 95%tile

Otis: I.Q. 125

Reading Comp: 90%tile

Here the test results consistently suggest that Mike has excellent potential. A quick check with teachers confirms this and produces the evidence that Mike is "goofing off," a fact I had already suspected. In this case, we naturally decided together that Mike should stay with the college course, repeat French 2, and grow up a little.

And so it goes. It's always a guessing game, but note that in the above cases, the counselor constantly looked for reasons to upgrade the quality of the program. Only when the evidence was beyond a reasonable doubt did we downgrade the program.

May I also add that in each case the decision was the pupil's. The counselor's role was to present facts, alternatives and possibilities. I'm not above applying a little subtle pressure in these cases if I feel the situation warrants it; but it is far better to "manipulate" the situation so that the student reaches the decision on his own. This is "directive" counseling as I see it.

There is another point where we refer to the test record, and that is when we discuss college choice with a student. For example, Dick's first choice is a very selective, highly competitive and demanding men's liberal arts college. His record is excellent, but he had to work hard to get his "B's" in English. In addition, his verbal I.Q. scores are just around 60%tile and he is a relatively slow reader (55%tile). This is reflected by a slightly above average verbal SAT score of 520. Under the circumstances, I feel Dick might have some difficulty in this type of school. I communicate this feeling to Dick, but I do not discourage him from applying. That's his decision to make. I just present the facts.

There are other occasions when test scores are used by counselors, but it is during these crucial decisions—program and post-high school planning—that we find them most useful.

What tests?

As to what tests to use, the woods are full of them. I don't think it matters what test you use, as long as you become familiar with it. It takes a few years to get used to a test. There are a few practical considerations that may be important. I would choose a test that is easy to administer to groups and one that doesn't take too much time. I would have them machine scored and the results reported on gummed labels for easy recording on the permanent record. I like a Scholastic Ability Test that produces a verbal and nonverbal score. I want the Reading Test to show speed, understanding, and degree of vocabulary development. Beyond this, it's a matter of wise use. I'm sure that, at this point, scores of experts are tearing their hair out in frenetic exasperation. I can't help it. After 20 years of using tests, this is the way I feel.

You may wonder at this rather cursory treatment of a problem that is the subject of many graduate courses and intensive research. We have tests now for everything from mechanical aptitude to the level of one's emotional involvement with "Winnie the Pooh." I'm probably reacting against a national effort to test, categorize, pigeon-hole and, in so many ways, limit the horizons of an unwitting citizenry. I rejoice at stories like that of the obscure clerk who enjoyed a meteoric rise to president of the board —after he had inadvertently stepped on his IBM card in his golf shoes. It loses in the translation, but the moral is there. It is a natural human impulse to find an easy way. Testing, on the surface, promises to offer easy solutions to many perplexing problems as to the complex matters of an individual. But despite years of research and libraries of theses, textbooks and assorted papers, tests continue to have their limitations. It is a great source of secret satisfaction to me that the human personality, vibrant and dynamic, still resists the impersonal probing of artificial devices which tend to limit or mold or predestine the individual in some way. I am obviously anti-guidance. I'm sorry, but I look upon the overemphasis of testing as an invasion of privacy. Let's make sure that our use of tests in guidance is not a limiting function, but a positive force. Let's emphasize what the test suggests is *possible* and cock a jaundiced eye at what the test indicates is impossible. So if you want to use a particular test, go ahead. I won't argue. It's not *what* test, but how you *use* it that's important.

Administering group tests

Testing large groups, like teaching, requires preparation, experience, and skill. There's a right way and a wrong way and, if we are to get the most out of the testing program, some care should be taken to insure that the test be given under the most advantageous conditions.

Breaking down a group into many small sections to be tested simultaneously has some obvious advantages—but the testing conditions are not apt to be uniform. I would almost prefer to sacrifice some physical advantages of the small group to gain uniformity. I would suggest that the same person administer the test in the same physical setting. However, other factors in the school may preclude this, and it's probably not that important.

Preparation for the test should include an orientation for the students. They should understand what the test is and how it will be used; they should be whipped into a frenzy of motivation. At least, we can pique their curiosity. Then, general directions can be given and a word about the technique of taking a standardized test can be offered. Since these are timed tests, advise students to work rapidly without hurrying. Suggest that they avoid spending too much time on any one question but to go on and, if they have time, return to it later. Advise them to avoid wild guesses but to go ahead on anything they *think* is right. Encourage them to relax and enjoy the test. After all, it's one of the few that they take in school where they can't fail!

The test administrator should read the manual of instructions thoroughly and follow directions carefully. It is imperative that he can be heard in all parts of the testing room. Use a reliable timing device. We use an interval timer which can be preset and has an alarm. The pupils must have adequate writing space. Finally, proctors are necessary to supervise the room and to handle the distribution and collection of test materials quickly. We seat pupils in rows behind each other and use those sitting on the aisles to collect and pass test materials in and out.

We count out the number of tests and answer sheets per row ahead of time, and this cuts the administration time to a minimum. It also helps to maintain a momentum and sustain a businesslike atmosphere. I hope I'm not dealing in trivia here, but I know that a well-organized test administration results in better performance by the students. They are very sensitive to the general atmosphere of the room at these times, since they are so keyed up.

Interpretation of tests to pupils

Students should be aware of their strengths and weaknesses if they are to arrive at any kind of realistic self-evaluation. They also should know the limitations of the measuring tools we are using. To this end, the counselor should schedule routine interviews with individual pupils to interpret test results. I like to talk in terms of percentiles since the concept of 50 as average is easily understood, while grade placement or I.Q. scores are subject to misunderstanding and are confusing. Except in rare cases, I do not think an I.Q. score should be disclosed even to parents. This is not because I feel there is anything sacred about an I.Q. score but, unless one knows the test and understands testing, I don't see that an I.Q. score means anything. Consequently, we deal with percentiles. I have mentioned before that, in the case of a scholastic aptitude test in the extremely low range, I prefer to take refuge in the term *low-average*. Again, the purpose is to avoid using the test as a limiting factor. I try to avoid planting or reinforcing the idea that the pupil is inadequate or unduly limited. With reading scores it is a different matter. This is a skill and pupils can accept the fact that they have a low reading ability. But the I.Q. test, to a pupil, has an authority and validity that we counselors know does not exist to the extent the pupil thinks. It attacks the ego—where it hurts. Another point—I refer always to Intelligence tests as Scholastic Aptitude tests, a more accurate and less alarming term.

The counselor should always consider the pupil when arriving at a test evaluation. Low test scores can be due to lack of motivation, immaturity, nervousness, low reading ability, low cultural background and illness during the test. Of course, all these factors except illness are valid reasons for poor school performance. So if we use the test as a predictor of academic success, the presence or absence of these factors makes no difference as far as the predictive value of the test is concerned. However, they make a significant difference in our evaluation of the ultimate potential of our counselees.

I think the practice of sending home reports of test results is debatable. Unless you can take the time to explain the significance of the results to parents, I doubt whether they mean much to them, and they probably cause more confusion than understanding. We've tried it in our school and abandoned it, primarily because of the time element. You might be able to circumvent some of these difficulties, and I know of many schools who send such a report home. I suspect the value of the report depends on the character of the community and the educational level of the parents.

Testing should be for the benefit of the entire school, and the results of testing should be readily available to teachers. We once published lists of pupils in the top and bottom quarters in I.Q. and reading tests. We abandoned this practice also because of the time element but are thinking of returning to the policy. Meanwhile, most teachers routinely examine the permanent records of their classroom students for this information. This is one instance where we could be of assistance to teachers by providing the information in a more readily available form.

College boards and similar necessary evils

Candidates for college come from a variety of secondary schools with widely varying standards and educational facilities. Therefore, colleges have found it necessary to use a common yardstick in measuring the scholastic potential of their candidates. Accordingly, most have adopted some national testing program. In the east, the College Board Exams (CEEB) of the Educational Testing Service are most commonly used, and have been for years. In addition, many colleges use the American College Testing Program (ACT).

THE CEEB TESTS

The tests of the College Entrance Examination Board are of two types:

1. The morning program consists of the Scholastic Aptitute Test (SAT), a three-hour examination which yields both a verbal and mathematical score. These scores range from 200 to 800. Medians vary from test to test, but 450 is roughly the verbal average and 510 the mathematical average.

2. The afternoon program consists of three Achievement Tests in specific subject material.

The Board supplies explanatory and interpretive booklets together with application blanks to the high school, free of charge upon request. The tests are scheduled for Saturdays throughout the year in November, December, January, March, May and July at numerous centers around the U.S. and abroad. The cost of the SAT is $5.00. The cost of one or more achievement tests is $7.50. All schools and colleges using this program require the SAT and, in many cases, the Achievement Tests as well. Candidates should consult the admission requirements of the various schools and colleges as listed in their current catalogs. Normally, the tests should be taken early in the senior year.

THE ACT

The American College Testing Program is a four-hour examination in the areas of English usage, Mathematical usage, Social Studies reading and Natural Science reading. Students voluntarily supply their most recent grades and on the basis of these and the test result, a predictive index of scholastic success is computed. This is presented along with percentile results in the four subject areas to the various colleges. The ACT program is given five times a year in October, December, February, May and August.

Much the same materials are provided to the individual and schools as by the CEEB. Testing centers are located all over the U.S. The cost to the pupil is $4.50.

We will return to the use and interpretation of these tests in a later chapter.

PRESSURES AND PROBLEMS

It is inevitable that the mounting pressure to gain admittance to the "prestige colleges" has resulted in some problems and misunderstanding. For instance, take the case of a fine small men's liberal arts college in New England. The admissions committee here must evaluate and process over 3000 applications for around 300 openings in the freshman class. The large majority of these candidates are honor students, clearly capable of undertaking the work successfully. Among them are scores of class presidents, student council leaders, crushing linebackers and expert trumpet players. So it becomes mandatory that the college board scores be given more importance than they deserve. As a result, a student needs to score unusually high to qualify for acceptance. In a sense, then, the board scores become a strong limiting factor. To give the admissions officers credit, they do not want this situation and do their best to evaluate the student as a human being rather than as a test score—as evidenced by the number of students admitted with relatively low test scores—students who stand out by reason of unique qualifications. Nevertheless, for most applicants the pressure to get high board scores is always there.

The result is overemphasis of tests and distorted educational goals and values. The student can be excused therefore if he is more concerned with getting a 650 Physics achievement score rather than becoming involved in Physics for its own sake. Of course, if he doesn't do the latter, he won't accomplish the former, and that is also part of the problem.

This situation has spawned a horde of tutoring schools and books all purporting to be able to improve the scores on these national examinations. I personally take a dim view of such artificial crutches. I would rather see a youngster read a good book. The Educational Testing Service has shown that all research points to the fact that no such tutoring has significantly increased the SAT score of the College Board Examinations. It is only an unwelcome overemphasis and puts more pressure on the student.

This does not mean that extra work in a subject will not pay off in higher Achievement Test scores, since these are examinations in the knowledge of subject material. Nor does it mean that a short course in how to take an examination—any examination with objective questions—cannot be of value. But this is not tutoring.

However, since there is no denying that national tests are important criteria in qualifying for college and school entrance, we make certain suggestions to insure that our students do their best on these tests. We are primarily concerned with the College Board Tests in our part of the country, so we urge juniors to take the PSAT in October. The PSAT (preliminary Scholastic Aptitude Test) is a two-hour abbreviated form of the SAT, administered in the school. We suggest this for two reasons: (1) It gives them experience in taking a form of the SAT, and (2) it gives us an idea of how they will perform in the SAT. This test was originally intended to supplant the practice of taking the SAT in the junior year, but we advise juniors to take the SAT anyway for additional experience and to give us more advance information. It is on the basis of this test and the academic record that we advise college choice in the fall. College candidates take the SAT and possibly the Achievement Tests in December of their senior year. Whereas we try to avoid overemphasis of the exams—in order to avoid putting emotional pressures on the youngsters—we sometimes suggest that those who received low scores in the junior year take the SAT both in December and January to give them the best chance to score well. This is primarily due to a policy of one of the local colleges that does have a cutoff point of 400. Most colleges, incidentally, do not have a rigid cutoff point, but many have an acceptable range, which amounts to much the same thing.

THE NATIONAL MERIT SCHOLARSHIP QUALIFYING TEST

This test, conducted by the Science Research Associates, Inc., is administered in most high schools to juniors. The test is a screening device for one of the largest national scholarship programs. It is highly competitive, but winners in need of financial aid are eligible to receive substantial scholarship help. It is a two-hour test with several subtests—English usage, Social Studies usage, Mathematics usage, Natural Science reading, and Word usage.

The test is given in March. Since only the top students in a general high school have a chance to qualify, we encourage only the top ten per cent of the class to register, although anyone may take the test. This is primarily because we lack adequate testing facilities for large groups, but also because I have not found the test particularly useful for guidance purposes. Qualifiers must take the December Board Exams in the senior year and the finalists are chosen on that basis together with their academic record. The usual explanatory materials are provided the school.

Conclusion

With this capsule description of tests and testing, I have attempted to point out the use and limitations of tests. As counselors, we find such measures useful. As humans conditioned to accepting test scores as authoritative, we should always be on our guard not to place too much value on tests. High scores are usually accurate measures—low scores can be way off! Our task is to use our best judgment in our evaluations, which should be based on as many factors as possible. Moreover, all evaluations should be periodically reviewed as our clients develop.

Bibliography of Tests

General Achievement

1. National Education Development Tests (NEDT) Grades 9-10.
2. IOWA Tests of Educational Development (ITED).
   Both from Science Research Associates, Inc., 259 East Erie St., Chicago, Illinois 60611

Intelligence

1. California Short-Form Test of Mental Maturity, 1963 Revision. California Test Bureau, Del Monte Research Park, Monterey, California 93940
2. Otis Quick Scoring Mental Ability Test, Gamma Test, Form AM. Harcourt, Brace and World, Inc., New York, N.Y.

Multi-Aptitude

1. Differential Aptitude Tests.

Psychological Corporation, 304 East 45th Street, New York, N.Y.   10017

Reading Comprehension

1. Cooperative Test Division, Educational Testing Service, Princeton, N.J.   08540; Berkeley, California   94701.

Interest and Personality Inventories

1. Kuder Preference Records; Form A—Personal, Form E—Vocational Interest.
Science Research Associates
2. California Test of Personality.
3. Occupational Interest Inventory.
Both California Test Bureau

4

Planning Effective Courses
for the High School
Years

A New Open Door Policy

One of our most important guidance tasks is to assist the pupil in planning his four-year high school program of courses. This involves decisions based on an understanding of the pupil's abilities and interests, as well as a knowledge of the requirements of schools and occupations. It is impossible to plan a program so successfully that it will not be changed in some manner. We are dealing with a rapidly developing, constantly changing individual. We are also using imperfect tools of evaluation. So flexibility and a readiness to adjust to change is necessary on the part of both counselor and client.

My personal philosophy of program planning is based on two convictions. The first is my belief that we should encourage all students, regardless of ability, to go on to some kind of further education beyond high school, if at all possible. The day of the unskilled worker is gone and there have never existed so many and varied opportunities for continuing one's education. There are limitations to this goal, of course. Some communities are located in areas distant from centers of education. Socio-economic backgrounds and lack of parental interest are other blocks. But where possible—and this applies even to trade and commercial course graduates who have already acquired some specialized skills—pupils should be pushed to the summit of their educational potential. High school should be a transfer rather than a terminal experience.

My second conviction is that we should encourage pupils to take those courses that will lead to the maximum opportunity within their ability ranges—regardless of their particular interests. For example, the college course, with some exceptions, offers the greatest opportunity. It opens all doors. Therefore, I encourage the girl who wishes to become a hairdresser to elect the college course if she has the capacity to do the work successfully. She can then be a hairdresser if she still wants to be—or a teacher, a nurse, a doctor or whatever future interests may direct. But if she elected only a general course as a preparation for hairdressing, she would be limited in her choice of post-high school experience in her senior year when mature judgment might result in a more ambitious choice of training.

It is obvious that very few youngsters know in junior high school what their ultimate occupational goal will be. Nor can we help them much to establish realistic vocational goals. Interest inventories, while helpful, are grossly inadequate. Kids at that age are so inexperienced, so lacking in knowledge of themselves or the world, that it seems ridiculous to expect them to be able to select a vocation with any degree of success. Many college seniors, in fact, cannot identify vocational interests with certainty.

Since the early vocational choices of pupils are subject to suspicion, it follows that pupil interests in general are a poor guide to course planning. At the same time, a tentative goal that is consistent with the pupil's abilities is probably a good incentive.

There are some practical considerations involved. The girl who may not be able to afford college is wise to plan a combination of college and business subjects which will give her an economic margin of safety by training her in salable skills, while keeping the door of higher education open in the event she can take advantage of it.

For those who apparently do not have the aptitude for this straight college course, it may be that they can profit from portions of it. We find many who can complete two years of college math, but who don't have the verbal facility required in college English and history. We find those who can handle a language, but who are poor math and science students. There is a certain amount of trial and error involved, but usually there is enough evidence in test results and the scholastic record to warrant the trial. Incidentally, the cultural backgrounds of pupils often impose more significant limitations than do I.Q. scores.

The flexible curriculum

All this requires a flexible program of studies. Such a curriculum, while a thorn in the side of the poor administrator who must do the yearly scheduling, is necessary if we are to recognize individual differences. There is always a strong temptation to group youngsters in various curricula based on ability and interests. It makes scheduling easier and satisfies the ever-present human impulse to categorize. But such a program is based on the assumption that an eighth grader can make such a curriculum choice with certitude or that we have measuring tools of high predictive accuracy. As I have stated above, neither student clairvoyancy nor fool-proof testing techniques have appeared on the guidance horizon to date. The obvious procedure, therefore, is to schedule on the basis of past performance, coupled with the cautious use of test scores, and then be prepared to change.

Likewise, the curriculum must allow for combinations of college, business and general courses. As an example, in our school of 1,000 pupils, we have around 800 different individual student programs each year. This sounds more extreme than it is. For instance, a junior in the college course could be taking one of four languages—or two languages—and be in different years of either than his classmates who might be taking different languages altogether. More to the point, we have general course boys taking college algebra, business course girls taking college English, and college course girls taking foods or clothing! In fact, we have all kinds of similar combinations which result in an habitual expression of reproach on the part of our long-suffering principal when late spring arrives and he must do the scheduling.

Such flexibility sometimes results in the tendency for pupils to attempt to change on impulse, to "shop" for courses. We try to keep them in clusters of courses that will qualify them for further school or good job placement. We discourage whims or unrealistic choices, while trying to satisfy real interests when it will not dilute the educational value of the individual's program. This approach also offers a chance to include exploratory courses. A college course boy might work in a course in bookkeeping in his senior year with the idea of following up an interest in accounting. Art, music, mechanical drawing and home economics are all examples of such exploratory courses, which are available to business and general students as well.

SCHEDULING EXAMPLES AND PRACTICE PROBLEMS

Let's discuss some concrete cases involving scheduling problems. A copy of a sample program of studies is reproduced in Figure 1. It is not offered as a model but merely as an example, and in this instance, for the purpose of working out some scheduling problems.

Figure 1

PROGRAM OF STUDIES—WESTFIELD HIGH SCHOOL

(Showing year in which each subject is normally offered first time)
* Indicates required subjects.
Each subject meets 5 times per week and carries 1 unit credit
(5-1) except as indicated.

9th Grade	10th Grade	11th Grade	12th Grade
* Eng. 1 (C or G)	* Eng. 2 (C or G)	* Eng. 3 (C or G)	* Eng. 4 (C or G)
* Geog.	* Hist. 2 (C or G) (World)	* Hist. 3 (C or G) (U.S.) Economics	* Prob. of Democ. (C or G)
* Alg. 1 (C or G)	Geom.	Alg. 2	Trig. & Solid Mod. Math.

Figure 1 (*cont.*)

* Gen. Sci. or Bio.	Bio. (Chem. if Bio. in 9th)	Chem. Phys. Sci. (Gen. Chem. & Physics)	Physics Advanced Bio.
Latin 1	Latin 2	Latin 3	
French 1	French 2	French 3	French 4
	Spanish 1	Spanish 2	Spanish 3
	German 1	German 2	German 3
Bus. Trng.	Bookkeeping 1	Bookkeeping 2	
	Typing 1 (5-½)	Typing 2 (5-½)	
	Coll. Typing (5-¼; ½ year)	Steno. 1	Steno. 2
		Off. Prac. 1	Off. Prac. 2
Home Economics	Foods 1	Foods 2	Home Management
	Clothing 1	Clothing 2	
Indus. Arts 1 (5-½) (Shop)	Indus. Arts 2 (5-½)	Indus. Arts 3 (5-½)	Indus. Arts 4 (5-½)
Art 1	Art 2	Art 3	Art 4
	Mech. Draw. 1 (5-½)	Mech. Draw. 2 (5-½)	
	Band (5-½)	Band (5-½)	
* Phys. Ed. 1 (2-¼)	* Phys. Ed. 2 (2-¼)	* Phys. Ed. 3 (2-¼)	* Phys. Ed. 4 (2-¼)
		Speech (2-¼)	Speech (2-¼)
			Driver Ed. (5-0) Certification for lower insurance rate.

You will note that the program of studies is divided rather loosely into college, business, and general courses. You will also note that the only ability grouping appears in college or general English, social studies, and algebra 1. The nature of such courses as physics, chemistry, geometry, and languages automatically puts them in a college preparatory status as far as the required scholastic ability is concerned. Such courses as general algebra 1, physical science, shop, foods, clothing, and home management are obviously within the ability range of the more scholastically limited student but are open to all students. Economics, mechanical drawing, art, band, and biology are available for both the college and noncollege student but are taught at a level that is within the ability of the general course student.

While it is impossible for someone unfamiliar with a school to evaluate a curriculum without knowing something about the course content and the particular standards of the teacher, I propose to demonstrate scheduling procedures with some actual cases.

The following are examples that came to us as transfers, and accordingly I had the opportunity to schedule the full four years. Ordinarily, of course, this is initiated by the junior high counselor.

Case 1

Mary G., 13 years old, I.Q. 114, middle-class family, well-adjusted, physically fit, tanned, blonde, with brown eyes.

Eighth grade record: English B+, Social Studies B, Math C+, Science A, Foods D.

Obviously a college prospect, I decide, even though her angel cake fell. Good academic record, good I.Q., no visible problems. So Mary, her family, and I schedule her courses as follows:

Freshman	*Sophomore*	*Junior*	*Senior*
Coll. Eng. 1	Coll. Eng. 2	Coll. Eng. 3	Coll. Eng. 4
Coll. Geog.	Coll. Hist. 2	Coll. Hist. 3	Coll. Prob.
Alg. 1	Geom.	Alg. 2	of Democ.
French 1	French 2	French 3	Mod. Math
Bio.	Coll. Typing	Economics	French 4
Phys. Ed. 1	Phys. Ed. 2	Phys. Ed. 3	Chem.
			Phys. Ed. 4

Note that we scheduled chemistry in the senior year instead of both chemistry and physics. With a stronger math record and higher I.Q., I would have suggested both. In this case, knowing the demands of the physics course, I felt that one science was more realistic. As it was, I had misgivings about the mod. math— a difficult course. Here's how it turned out:

Freshman		*Sophomore*	
Coll. Eng. 1	B	Coll. Eng. 2	C
Coll. Geog.	B	Coll. Hist. 2	B
Alg. 1	C	Geom. (dropped)	
French 1	C	Alg. 1	B
Bio.	B	French 2	C
Phys. Ed. 1	C	Typing	C
		Phys. Ed. 2	C

Junior		*Senior*	
Coll. Eng. 3	C	Coll. Eng. 4	B
Coll. Hist. 3	C	Coll. Prob. of Democ.	C
Geom.	D	Alg. 2	C
French 3	B	French 4	C
Economics	A	Chem.	D
Phys. Ed. 3	B	Phys. Ed. 4	C

With no particular warning, Mary found herself weak in math. In this case there was no way of predicting this. She dropped geometry in the middle of the second term and reviewed algebra 1. Then she passed geometry with a high D and labored mightily for a C in algebra 2. As a matter of interest, she entered a state college for teachers, taught very successfully for two years and is now the mother of two tanned, blonde, and brown-eyed toddlers. But her angel cake is still falling.

Lesson: I don't think that the fact she is a poor geometry student bothers her husband one bit!

Case 2

Theresa K., 14 years old, I.Q. 109, reading 60%tile, family of limited income, 5 younger brothers and sisters, good worker, well-adjusted, mature, her family wants the business course for her.

Eighth grade record: English C+, Social Studies C, Math B+, Science C, Art C, Foods A.

I consider the possibility of encouraging college English and social studies but discard the idea in view of the "C's" in eighth grade. However, we decide to elect algebra 1 and geometry along with the regular stenographic course as follows:

Freshman	Sophomore	Junior	Senior
Gen. Eng. 1	Gen. Eng. 2	Gen. Eng. 3	Gen. Eng. 4
Gen. Geog.	Gen. Hist. 2	Gen. Hist. 3	Gen. Prob. of
Alg. 1	Geom.	Off. Prac. 1	Democ.
Gen. Sci.	Bookkeeping 1	Steno. 1	Off. Prac. 2
Bus. Trng.	Typing 1	Typing 2	Steno. 2
Phys. Ed. 1	Phys. Ed. 2	Phys. Ed. 3	Home
			Management
			Phys. Ed. 4

Here's how this one turned out.

Freshman		Sophomore	
Gen. Eng. 1	B	Gen. Eng. 2	C
Gen. Geog.	B	Coll. Hist. 2	B
Alg. 1	B	Geom.	C
Gen. Sci.	C	Bookkeeping 1	B
Bus. Trng.	A	Typing 1	A
Phys. Ed. 1	C	Phys. Ed. 2	C

Junior		Senior	
Coll. Eng. 3	C	Coll. Eng. 4	C
Coll. Hist. 3	C	Coll. Prob. of Democ.	B
French 1	C	French 2	B
Steno. 1	A	Steno. 2	B
Typing 2	B	Chem.	C
Phys. Ed. 3	D	Phys. Ed. 4	C

Theresa did well enough her freshman year to warrant giving her a try at the college course and with her ambition and industry, she did quite well. Here is a case where the test scores were inaccurate as predictors of scholastic success—one of many such cases I may add. She was able to finance the local state college and is now a successful teacher. She might have been as successful as a secretary had she wished.

Lesson: Be ready to adjust up as well as down—although all cases won't turn out as well as this one.

Case 3

George M., 13 years old, I.Q. 128, reading 85%tile, middle-class family, shy, immature, uncommunicative.

Eighth grade record: English A, Social Studies C+, Math B, Science B, Shop C.

A clearly capable boy with a good record and high test scores, so we schedule as follows:

Freshman	Sophomore	Junior	Senior
Coll. Eng. 1	Coll. Eng. 2	Coll. Eng. 3	Coll. Eng. 4
Geog.	Coll. Hist. 2	Coll. Hist. 3	Coll. Prob. of
Alg. 1	Geom.	Alg. 2	Democ.
French 1	French 2	French 3	Mod. Math or
Gen. Sci.	Coll. Typing	Chem.	Trig.
Phys. Ed. 1	Phys. Ed. 2	Phys. Ed. 3	French 4
			Physics
			Phys. Ed. 4

But here's how he performed:

Freshman		Sophomore	
Coll. Eng. 1	B	Coll. Eng. 2	C
Geog.	B	Coll. Hist. 2	C
Alg. 1	B	Geom.	C
French 1	C	French 2	E
Gen. Sci.	B	Coll. Typing	D
Phys. Ed. 1	B	Phys. Ed. 2	B

Junior		Senior	
Coll. Eng. 3	D	Coll. Eng. 4	D
Coll. Hist. 3	D	Coll. Prob. of Democ.	D
Alg. 2	E	Alg. 2 (repeat)	C
French 2		Physics	E
(repeat)	D	Phys. Ed. 4	C
Chem.	D		
Phys. Ed. 3	B		

George was hit by both the discovery of girls—always an unsettling experience—and a desire to be one of the gang. He ran around with the older, more sophisticated lads and spent less and less time with the books. While always pleasant, George never really became friendly with me—or with any adult. Under the circumstances, his academic standing dropped slowly but surely as his family's blood pressure rose in inverse proportion. So I struck out again. However, George spent two happy years in our armed forces and emerged a different boy—mature, self-confident and enlightened. He is currently doing well in a transfer course at a junior college.

Lesson: It's never too late.

It may strike you that behind all this scheduling is the strong directing hand of the counselor. And it's true that here is a situation where the counselor should influence and direct. This is a vital point in the educational process, and who but the counselor knows his own curriculum, and at the same time, the requirements of various schools and occupations? Certainly not most parents. So, although the wish of the student is the final word, he will probably agree with the counselor once the reasons and alternatives are explained.

Another conclusion that the reader may reach is that, with transfers from other school systems, we don't have much to go on when attempting to evaluate a student's scholastic capacity. This is true. We have to depend on the permanent record—an impersonal document which cannot reflect the flesh and blood individual or the quality of his preparation adequately. With kids from our own system, we depend on the eighth grade counselor to point him in the right direction, and then it is up to us to watch over the pupil like a mother hen—always looking for ways to upgrade his program. After the first half-year in high school, we usually have a fair idea of how he operates, his strengths and limitations. Then we can schedule the last three years with more confidence. But even then, there are surprises.

At this point, I would like to offer the reader a temporary job in our school. I propose to sketch in the background facts of some actual cases taken from our records and let you try your hand at scheduling these total strangers. My purpose here is to demonstrate to the reader the necessity of knowing his own school's curriculum, the requirements of schools and occupations, and the intellectual capacity and motivation of his counselees.

Before trying the scheduling problems, I suggest that the reader study the instructions to eighth graders in Figure 2, following, as well as the sample program of studies (Figure 1) with the explanatory information. Again I remind you that this is not the ideal program of studies. We hope to improve it in the future.

Figure 2

INSTRUCTIONS TO EIGHTH GRADERS

I. General Requirements for Graduation:

Graduation requirements are of two kinds.

1. Points: Passing each full course counts 1 point toward graduating. Some courses, such as typing, count ½ point. Refer to the four-year curriculum sheet. 16 points are required for graduation. Promotion requirements are as follows:

To Sophomore	4 points
To Junior	7 points
To Senior	11 points
To Graduate	16 points

2. Course Requirements: 4 years of English, 4 years of social studies, 1 year of mathematics, 1 year of science must be passed by everyone in order to graduate. Physical education must be taken each year unless excused by a doctor's note.

II. Suggestions for Course Selection:

We offer courses of study labeled *college, general,* and *business.* Actually there is a great amount of flexibility allowed in the individual's choice of subjects, and combinations of college and business courses are common. For example, general course students may take college math or science. We are more concerned with challenging the abilities of students than with keeping to rigid course curricula.

Pupils should elect at least four full credit courses or three full credit and two half credit courses a year for a total of 4 points. Also include physical education each year. We recommend against more than five 1-point subjects a year in all but a few cases.

III. Curricula Descriptions:

1. General Curriculum ("G" Courses)

The general curriculum does not point in any specific direction as far as vocation or post-high school education is concerned. Nevertheless, a student taking this course is eligible for further school beyond high school. Students graduating from this course can enter technical schools, business schools, and specialty schools of all kinds. With each passing year, students find post-high school training more important, and more students continue their education after high school graduation.

Required: English 1G, 2G, 3G, 4G

Figure 2 (*cont.*)

Geography, History 2G, 3G, Problems of Democracy 4G
Physical Education 1, 2, 3, 4
A science course
A math course

Electives: Any combination of courses to add up to the required 16 points. Following are some sample combinations.

The student interested in the technical—mechanical—scientific fields may select from the following:

English 1G, 2G, 3G, 4G
Geography, History 2G, 3G, Problems of Democracy 4G
General Math, General Algebra 1, General Math 2
(or College Algebra 1, Geometry, Algebra 2 if ability permits or any combination of the above. These must be taken in sequence, however.)
General Science, Biology, Physical Science
Mechanical Drawing 1, 2
Shop 1, 2, 3, 4
College Typing (½ year)
Physical Education 1, 2, 3, 4

The girl interested in homemaking may select from the following:

English 1G, 2G, 3G, 4G
Geography, History 2G, 3G, Problems of Democracy 4G
Foods 1, 2
Clothing 1, 2, 3
Home Management 1 (Senior year only)
Typing 1, 2
Office Practice 1
General Science, Biology
General Math, General Algebra 1, General Math 2
Physical Education 1, 2, 3, 4

Naturally, a student cannot take all of these subjects. College math should be taken in place of general math, if the pupil has the required ability. The typing and office practice are suggested as valuable job-training skills.

In both of the combinations, art may be included in any or all of the four years.

2. College Curriculum ("C" Courses)

College requirements vary. For this reason we urge those with the necessary ability (average of "B" or better) to take the regular courses outlined below. It will lead to the largest number of choices.

Figure 2 (cont.)

English 1C, 2C, 3C, 4C
Geography, History 2C, 3C, Problems of Democracy 4C
College Algebra 1, Geometry, Algebra 2
Language 1, 2, 3
Chemistry or Physics
Physical Education 1, 2, 3, 4
Electives may include a fourth year of math, science, or language.

Biology for students with excellent records may be elected for the freshman year. These students may take chemistry in the sophomore year, if desired.

Engineering colleges have slightly different requirements:

English 1C, 2C, 3C, 4C
Geography, History 2C, 3C, Problems of Democracy 4C
College Algebra 1 (in ninth grade), Geometry, Algebra 2, Trig
    & Solid Geometry
Chemistry & Physics
Physical Education 1, 2, 3, 4
Electives

No language is required, but two years are strongly recommended. Mechanical drawing may be substituted for the third year of the language.

Business colleges prefer the regular college course, but many would accept a program like the following:

English 1C, 2C, 3C, 4C
Geography, History 2C, 3C, Problems of Democracy 4C
College Algebra 1, Geometry
Biology, Chemistry or Physics
Typing 1
Electives from the college or business courses.

State colleges for teaching require the following:

English 1C, 2C, 3C, 4C
Geography, History 2C, 3C, Problems of Democracy 4C
College Algebra 1, Geometry
Biology, Chemistry or Physics
Electives

If the pupil plans to get an A.B. in a major subject and minor in education, two years of a language are required. Although the colleges have accepted students in the past with general English and history courses, we feel that a teacher candidate would be seriously handi-

Figure 2 (*cont.*)

capped in competition for entrance to these schools without a solid
college preparatory course.

3. *Business Curriculum*

This curriculum will prepare students for bookkeeping, accounting,
secretarial and general clerical schools and occupations.

    English 1G, 2G, 3G, 4G
    Geography, History 2G, 3G, Problems of Democracy 4G
    Bookkeeping 1, 2
    Typing 1, 2
    Stenography 1, 2
    Office Practice 1, 2
    Physical Education 1, 2, 3, 4

From this offering pupils may select certain combinations according
to their interests and abilities. Pupils with ability should select college
English and history although it is not required. Neither stenography 1
nor office practice 1 can be elected until the junior year.

We urge that two or even three years of mathematics be elected,
particularly if accounting is the goal. In all, 16 units including electives from any field (languages, science, art, etc.) are required. Here
are some sample courses of study:

Bookkeeping & Accounting

English 1, 2, 3, 4
Geography, History 2, 3, Prob-
    lems of Democracy 4
Bookkeeping 1, 2
Typing 1, 2
Office Practice 1, 2
Alg. 1, Geometry
Physical Education 1, 2, 3, 4
Electives

Secretarial

English 1, 2, 3, 4
Geography, History 2, 3, Prob-
    lems of Democracy 4
Bookkeeping 1
Typing 1, 2
Office Practice 1
Stenography 1, 2
Physical Education 1, 2, 3, 4
Electives

General Clerical

English 1, 2, 3, 4
Geography, History 2, 3, Problems of Democracy 4
Bookkeeping 1, 2
Typing 1, 2
Office Practice 1, 2
Physical Education 1, 2, 3, 4
Electives

Figure 2 (*cont.*)

Pupils planning to take stenography should be at least "C" English students and above average in scholastic ability in general.

4. *Collegiate Program of Nursing*

If you are planning to take the degree granting course in college, take the regular college course, including three years of math, two years of a foreign language, and a college preparatory laboratory science—chemistry and/or physics. Biology is also strongly recommended.

5. *Three-Year Hospital School of Nursing*

If you are planning on a three-year hospital school of nursing, the college preparatory course is preferred. Many three-year schools of nursing want their prospective students to have two years of college preparatory math, such as algebra 1 and geometry. Chemistry and biology should be taken. Two years of Latin or any language is desirable.

Inasmuch as hospital schools of nursing vary somewhat in their requirements, it would be wise for nursing candidates to become familiar with the requirements of the school of nursing in which they are interested.

As for schools of practical nursing, high school graduation is essential. It would be wise to include biology and other sciences if possible.

Since the reader has no way of knowing the relative difficulty of certain courses, the following table is intended to aid in scheduling within the sample curriculum. This is obvious oversimplification but may help.

Most Rigorous	*Difficult*	*Less Difficult*
Trig & Solid	Coll. Eng. 1 & 2	Economics
Physics	Coll. Geog., Coll.	Bio.
Chem.	Hist. 2	Off. Prac.
Alg. 2	Languages	Bookkeeping
Mod. Math	Coll. Alg. 1	Gen. Alg.
Coll. Eng 3 & 4	Geom.	
Coll. Hist. 3 &	Steno.	
Coll. Prob. of		
Democ. 4		
Advanced		
Bio.		

The rest are either paced for the slower students or are obviously "skill" courses demanding special interests or talents. In either case, the general course student is ordinarily capable of handling these courses as well as those in column 3 and occasionally, column 2. You will probably guess that the divisions are made on the basis of the degree of abstract reasoning and verbal facility involved and, as we go down the scale, the capacity to memorize. In different schools, different patterns would hold true somewhat.

Just to make it more interesting, insert a letter grade for each course according to your evaluation of each pupil. Then compare your prediction with the actual record beginning on page 76. Schedule for four years on a seven period/day basis. If you score over 50%, send us your credentials. We need you!

Case 4

Susan L. 13 yrs. old; I.Q. 125; Reading, 80%tile. Mature, attractive, serious worker. Family wants college for her.

8th grade record: English B, Arithmetic A, Social Studies A, Science A, Music A, Art A.

Case 5

Christine L. 14 yrs. old; I.Q. 96; Reading 50%tile. Mature, dependable. Wants to be a secretary.

8th grade record: English C, Arithmetic C, Social Studies C, Science C, Music B, Art B.

Case 6

George P. 14 yrs. old; I.Q. 105; Reading 50%tile. Immature but conforming. Wants college course—no idea of future career.

8th grade record: English D, Arithmetic E, Social Studies C, Science B, Music B, Art B.

Case 7

Alice M. 14 yrs. old; I.Q. 99; Reading 41%tile. Immature, slightly rebellious daughter of a strict family. May be interested in an art career. Doesn't want Business.

8th grade record: English C, Arithmetic C, Social Studies C, Science D, Art A, Music C.

Case 8

Robert M. 13 yrs. old; I.Q. 111; Reading 55%tile. Alert, conscientious, shy, youngest of four brothers. Intends to go to college.

8th grade record: English B, Arithmetic B, Social Studies B, Science B, Music B, Art D.

Case 9

Helen P. 14 yrs. old; I.Q. 89; Reading 95%tile. Alert, good worker. Undecided on career.

8th grade record: English B, Arithmetic B, Social Studies B, Science B, Music C, Art C.

Case 10

Ellen P. 13 yrs. old; I.Q. 98; Reading 55%tile. Immature, attractive, conforms. Thinks she might want to work in an office.

8th grade record: English D, Arithmetic C, Social Studies C, Science C, Music C, Art B.

Case 11

Linda R. 14 yrs. old; I.Q. 88; Reading 41%tile. Immature, quiet, introverted—comes from lower class family. Possibly office work.

8th grade record: English D, Arithmetic D, Social Studies D, Science D, Music C, Art C.

Case 12

Betty P. 13 yrs. old; I.Q. 117; Reading 66%tile. Mature, active, gregarious, a leader, good worker. Wants nursing.

8th grade record: English B, Arithmetic A, Social Studies A, Science A, Music B, Art C.

The following are the actual records of *Cases 4–12*. How good a swami were you?

Case 4.   Susan L.

Coll. Eng. 1	B	Coll. Eng. 2	B
Geog.	A	Coll. Hist. 2	A
Bio.	A	Chem.	B
Alg. 1	B	Geom.	A
French 1	C	French 2	B
Phys. Ed. 1	B	Coll. Typing	C
		Phys. Ed. 2	B

Coll. Eng. 3	A	Coll. Eng. 4	B
Coll. Hist. 3	A	Coll. Prob. of Democ.	B
Alg. 2	B	Mod. Math	B
French 3	A	French 4	A
Spanish 1	A	Spanish 2	A
Phys. Ed. 3	B	Phys. Ed. 4	B

Susan did well, as expected. She preferred languages to science, thus no Physics. She is currently doing well in a state college.

Case 5.   Christine L.

Gen. Eng. 1	C	Gen. Eng. 2	C
Geog.	C	Gen. Hist. 2	B
Gen. Sci.	D	Bookkeeping 1	C
Gen. Math	D	Foods 1	B
Bus. Trng.	B	Typing 1	C
Phys. Ed.	B	Phys. Ed. 2	C

Gen. Eng. 3	B	Gen. Eng. 4	B
Gen. Hist. 3	D	Gen. Prob. of Democ.	C
Off. Prac. 1	B	Off. Prac. 2	B
Steno. 1	B	Steno. 2	B
Typing 2	C	Home Management	B
Phys. Ed. 3	B	Phys. Ed. 4	C

Chris did better as she went along. She is currently employed as a secretary in a local office.

Case 6. George P.

Coll. Eng. 1	D	Coll. Eng. 2	D
Geog.	C	Coll. Hist. 2	D
Gen. Sci.	B	Bio.	C
Gen. Math	C	Alg. 1	D
Bus. Trng.	C	Spanish 1	E
Phys. Ed. 1	C	Phys. Ed. 2	C
Gen. Eng. 3	C	Gen. Eng. 4	B
Gen. Hist. 3	C	Gen. Prob. of Democ.	C
Phys. Sci.	B	Chem.	D
Geom.	C	Alg. 2	D
Mech. Draw. 1	C	Mech. Draw. 2	C
Phys. Ed. 3	C	Phys. Ed. 4	C

George did not do well enough in the college course his sophomore year to continue. However, we kept the math on a hunch. Surprisingly enough, he did well enough to get through algebra 2 and chemistry, no easy task. He is currently enrolled in a two-year technical school and doing well. It was mostly a matter of growing up.

Case 7. Alice M.

Gen. Eng. 1	D	Gen. Eng. 2	D
Geog.	C	Gen. Hist. 2	C
Gen. Sci.	C	Bio.	C
Gen. Math	C	Alg. 1	E
Art 1	B	Art 2	C
Phys. Ed. 1	C	Phys. Ed. 2	C
Gen. Eng. 3	C	Gen. Eng. 4	C
Gen. Hist. 3	C	Gen. Prob. of Democ.	C
Phys. Sci.	D	Economics	B
Gen. Alg. 1	C	Alg. 1 (repeat)	C
Art 3	B	Home Management	C
Typing 1	C	Typing 2	C
Phys. Ed. 3	C	Phys. Ed. 4	C

After drifting around, she finally decided on an art career, took summer courses in English and geometry after her senior year and is enrolled in a junior college art curriculum. This is another of those students who must grow up. There is no way of anticipating how they will develop.

Case 8.   Robert M.

Coll. Eng. 1	B	Coll. Eng. 2	C
Geog.	A	Coll. Hist. 2	B
Gen. Sci.	A	Bio.	B
Alg. 1	B	Geom.	B
Latin 1	C	Spanish 1	B
Phys. Ed. 1	A	Phys. Ed. 2	B
Coll. Eng. 3	C	Coll. Eng. 4	C
Coll. Hist. 3	B	Coll. Prob. of Democ.	C
Chem.	B	Physics	C
Alg. 2	C	Alg. 2 (repeat)	B
Spanish 2	C	Spanish 3	B
Phys. Ed. 3	B	Phys. Ed. 4	B

Robert did about as expected. You couldn't have anticipated the sudden switch to Spanish, which was done in the ninth grade in junior high (we're now in a 3–3 system), and I don't know the reason for it. We like to keep them in the same language for at least two years, preferably three or four.

Case 9.   Helen P.

Gen. Eng. 1	B	Gen. Eng. 2	C
Geog.	A	Gen. Hist. 2	C
Gen. Sci.	B	Bookkeeping 1	B
Gen. Math	B	Clothing 1	C
Phys. Ed. 1	C	Typing 1	C
		Phys. Ed. 2	C
Gen. Eng. 3	A	Gen. Eng. 4	B
Gen. Hist. 3	B	Gen. Prob. of Democ.	B
Bookkeeping 2	A	Art 1	B
Alg. 1	A	Geom.	B
Foods 1	C	Home Management	B
Phys. Ed. 3	C	Phys. Ed. 4	C

Here is a case where we were blind to her potential. Overly influenced by the I.Q. score, I should have been alerted by the freshman year achievement and encouraged her to take a college course. At least we worked in the math. Helen developed an interest in interior decorating and should be at a good four-year college. Instead she is an apprentice in a large department store learning interior decoration at a lower level than she deserves. Bad mark for the counselor on this one! Incidentally, subsequent testing came up with an I.Q. of 112.

Case 10. Ellen P.

Gen. Eng. 1	D	Gen. Eng. 2	D
Geog.	C	Gen. Hist. 2	D
Gen. Sci.	B	Bookkeeping 1	E
Gen. Math	C	Foods 1	D
Art 1	B	Typing 1	D
Phys. Ed. 1	C	Phys. Ed. 2	C
Gen. Eng. 3	D	Gen. Eng. 4	C
Gen. Hist. 3	D	Gen. Prob. of Democ.	C
Off. Prac. 1	C	Off. Prac. 2	C
Foods 2	D	Home Management	C
Typing 2	C	Phys. Ed. 4	D
Phys. Ed. 3	C		

Ellen did somewhat better her senior year, and we were able to place her in a general clerical job. She too grew up finally—they usually do.

Case 11. Linda R.

Gen. Eng. 1	C	Gen. Eng. 2	D
Geog.	D	Gen. Hist. 2	E
Gen. Sci.	D	Bookkeeping 1	E
Gen. Math	D	Typing 1	E
Bus. Trng.	D	Foods 1	E
Phys. Ed. 1	C	Phys. Ed. 2	C
Gen. Eng. 3	D	Gen. Eng. 4	C
Gen. Hist. 3	D	Gen. Prob. of Democ.	D
Bookkeeping 1		Economics	D
(repeat)	D	Home Management	C
Typing (repeat)	C	Foods 2	D
Foods 1		Phys. Ed. 4	C
(repeat)	D		
Phys. Ed. 3	D		

Linda just made it! As a matter of fact she was ready to drop out of school at the end of her sophomore year, but we talked her out of it and persuaded her to take the history 2 make-up course in the summer. Linda gradually gained self-confidence but was one of my steady customers throughout school; in fact, she hugged me in the corridor on graduation day. I like to think we helped her.

Case 12.   Betty P.

Coll. Eng. 1	B	Coll. Eng. 2	B
Geog.	B	Coll. Hist. 2	A
Bio.	A	Chem.	C
Alg. 1	A	Geom.	E
Latin 1	A	Latin 2	C
Phys. Ed. 1	C	Phys. Ed. 2	B
Coll. Eng. 3	B	Coll. Eng. 4	B
Coll. Hist. 3	B	Coll. Prob. of Democ.	C
Spanish 1	A	Spanish 2	A
Geom.	B	Alg. 2	C
Latin 3	C	Economics	A
Phys. Ed. 3	B	Phys. Ed. 4	B

Note that Betty elected the college course at our suggestion even though it was not necessary for the R.N. training. She might have changed her mind; that she didn't is unimportant. I can't account for the trouble with geometry. Betty was accepted by a good hospital for nursing training—she'll be a wonderful nurse.

How did you fare? If your original program was different from mine, don't despair. On the contrary, *your* program might have been much better.

The most obvious lesson to be learned from this exercise is that it is impossible to predict an eighth or even ninth grader's progress. Test scores, while useful, are inaccurate and inadequate measures. The academic record is more indicative, but even there we find radical departures from the expected. There is no way of knowing whether or not a boy will be hit by "teen-itis" in his junior year—the "year of the car." On the other hand, we cannot anticipate the development of self-confidence and maturity on the part of the "late bloomer."

COURSE ADJUSTMENTS

In my school, we have built some elasticity into our programming with the introduction of a general algebra course. This works well for the calculated risk who wants to try his hand at college math. If he is good enough in general algebra, we'll transfer him to college algebra during the first half-year. Otherwise, if he is reasonably successful, we will encourage him to try college algebra the following year. He gets but one credit for the two courses, but can then continue on to further math courses as his performance warrants.

At any time during the first half-year, the policy of our school allows us to transfer pupils from college to general courses and vice versa. We try to hold to a policy of requiring reasonable effort before allowing pupils to switch. This discourages the "goof off" who wants an easy way out.

We also have a policy of transferring pupils during the year from an advanced course to the previous year of the course for review purposes. Thus an unsuccessful geometry student could switch to algebra during the first half-year. This has the advantage of reviewing the algebra (if he wishes to ultimately take algebra 2) and gives him a good start on geometry, which he can take again the following year. This policy has proven very effective for slower students who are not mature enough to handle these important courses in the early years of high school.

Curiously, repeating language courses often does not work out well. I assume that, in these cases, the youngster tends to coast through the part he already knows and well into that portion he didn't learn in the first place—with disastrous results.

The result of these policies is a higher rate of course changes than might be normal at many schools. But I think it is justified by the opportunities afforded. We must remember that it is the teachers who suffer from such changes. Rank books, seating plans, etc., are in a shambles, and teachers are justifiably irked at indiscriminate changes—or any changes at all—unless they are consulted. *All* course adjustments should be made with the understanding and consent of the classroom teacher.

Much of what I say about course changes would apply to any school. However, some of the things that we do successfully in our school might not work in another because of the peculiarities of the course and the philosophy of the teacher involved. I cited these specific courses to illustrate the advantage of a flexible curriculum in giving each pupil the maximum opportunity for educational growth.

SOME RANDOM THOUGHTS ON PROGRAMMING

It is my observation that far too little time and thought is spent on this business of scheduling courses. The practice of sending the eighth grade youngster home with a sheet of explanatory material, and then expecting him and his family to come up with a reasonable program plan is unrealistic. Somewhere in the process, the counselor should sit down with the pupil and discuss the possibilities. The ideal procedure is for the counselor and pupil to arrive jointly at a tentative plan for parental approval. Adjustments can be made if the parents wish something changed, but in this case the counselor has a contact with the parent and a chance to explain things. We ask that a four-year plan be made out, although we are primarily interested in the first year of high school (in a four-year high school). Although we know the program will be changed from time to time, we think it's good policy to make the pupil think ahead.

As a general guideline, I suggest aiming high. If a youngster looks as though he could benefit from the college course even though there may be reservations in our minds, we should encourage it. It would be unfair to him to do otherwise. At the same time, this policy runs the risk of diluting the college courses with a disproportionate number of slower students. This can only result in a lowering of standards, since it puts a subtle pressure on a teacher who is forced to "teach down." Somewhere in between there is a middle road. It helps to let a teacher know which of his pupils are among these calculated risks.

By now the reader should realize that I feel mathematics is a very desirable course, particularly for boys. I try to work in as much college math as the student can handle. I would like to insert another commercial for the general algebra course. This course, taught by an enthusiastic teacher at a much slower tempo than the college divisions and omitting the "abstract problem" work, is an excellent tryout course for the question marks. Also, it is surprising how much the slower student can do with an expert teacher. Even the below average student can do most of the mechanical manipulation. So many schools and jobs require math —so many doors are opened to the youngster that has this background!

The timing of course changes is sometimes a matter of judgment. In our school, we register all students shortly after the mid-year term, in February. This amounts to a preliminary registration, but allows the administration to line things up for the next year. In May and June we see all the underclassmen to check on their programs; obvious adjustments are made then. For some cliff-hangers, we have to wait until marks close in June.

No one is allowed to change courses in September unless there has been a change of status during the summer because of summer school. Our policy is to wait until after the first term before making many changes, unless we find a youngster well over his head after the first few weeks. There are some exceptions. We do not make out the rank sheets until after the first term. Until that point, a student taking a course may drop it and it will not appear on the record. This gives the pupil an opportunity to try a rigorous course and not be penalized if it doesn't work out. After the first term it will appear on the record as "dropped—E." There is a limit to this, of course, if we are to be fair to everybody. We try to effect the change, if necessary, as early as possible. I suppose this policy could be subject to debate. I view it as another bit of flexibility which encourages a student to reach up. It does not seem to result in either a lowering of standards, or an invitation to drop. As with all changes, we insist on a reasonable effort on the part of the pupil. Also, as with all changes, the pupil must have the recommendation of the classroom teacher in order to withdraw from the course.

It is always wise to obtain the parent's consent on all changes. I have found, to my sorrow, that kids can't be trusted to give the word to parents, so we use a "request to change" form on which the teacher and counselor can make brief remarks and which the parent can sign to signify approval. This may seem trivial but it is important. I still bear the bruises from parents who learned, at the end of the year, that Willie dropped chemistry in April. Most changes are worth a phone call, but use the form anyway so there is a record of parental approval.

The use of this "request to change" form also discourages needless changes. It gives one a convenient defense against the youngster who, after three weeks of home management, decides she is never going to be married and doesn't need the course. It is always a battle to keep kids from taking the easy way out. A bit of irony: The same girl who decided against marriage was pregnant in January and wed in April—hardly to be considered a towering success for guidance on anyone's part—and certainly not the intent of the home management course.

Ability grouping, tracks, etc.

While not an expert, I am unalterably opposed to ability groupings in high school other than the broad division into college and general English and social studies. This seems to be justifiable since the nature of the two courses are different enough to warrant the split. Even this I consider a necessary evil. For the rest, the difficulty of the course should determine who takes it. In our school, almost any pupil who is willing to work can pass general algebra, but only those gifted with the power of abstract reasoning and who are reasonably quick learners can master college algebra. This amounts to an ability grouping, but it is an individual rather than a group differentiation.

My reasoning behind this has nothing to do with the democratic process and equal rights but rather with the inherent educational weakness of such practices. The purpose behind ability groupings is worthy enough. Supposedly, the high ability pupil progresses faster while the low ability pupil is given different material, easier to master, thus nurturing a feeling of self-confidence and "ego-gratification." It has been my experience and that of teachers that it doesn't work out that way in practice. The fast student doesn't seem to progress that much more rapidly and the slow student finds himself labeled so and often becomes firmly mired in the morass of apathy and boredom. The feeling of teachers who have taught these slow classes is that, with the brighter kids siphoned off, the remainder react negatively to the lack of stimulation and challenge. Even within the broad grouping of college and general English, this effect is noticed. Like Communism, ability grouping looks good on paper but doesn't work in practice. Human beings need competition and incentives.

Another criticism of ability grouping is that the youngsters are grouped according to questionable criteria—test scores and the academic record. We have already seen that these measures are imperfect, but they are the only ones we have. To put a child into a low-ability compartment on such a basis is comparable to sentencing a man on circumstantial evidence.

The most insidious effect of ability groupings, however, is the tendency to keep a child boxed up in his compartment. The youngster finds himself labeled *slow*, accepts the label and seldom fights his way out. The administration also accepts the label and the child becomes doomed to a watered-down, lifeless and boring educational treadmill. Under these conditions, secondary school becomes a four-year sentence rather than an opportunity. There may be schools where skillful, imaginative and enthusiastic teachers can counteract these evils. I have yet to talk with a teacher who would not prefer classes of mixed ability where selection of pupils depended on the demands of the course rather than administrative structuring.

The alternative to ability grouping lies in the school's willingness to offer a wide variety of courses satisfying the range of interests and abilities of the general high school student body. Advanced placement courses or accelerated courses will challenge the gifted student. Less demanding courses, but not necessarily the same courses watered down, should be offered to the slower student, along with plenty of opportunity to try the more difficult courses. I have always felt that the general course students are capable of much more than most teachers think, but it takes a skillful and patient teacher to challenge them. Too many of these students have bought the idea that they are indeed "stupid."

My conclusion, shared by most teachers with whom I have discussed this problem, is that, while we have to recognize the limitations and strength of pupils, we should not categorize, label or sort them in any kind of routine, mechanical manner. We should have no compartments in our schools—no dead ends—only open doors with signs saying "this way up."

Summary

This chapter has shown that the task of course selection and adjustment is important enough to warrant the expenditure of considerable time and effort by the counselor. The student's individual program of studies determines the nature and quality of his education. But for most, quality education just doesn't happen automatically. It is in this area that the alert counselor can best justify his existence by providing a strong guiding hand, both at the planning stage and subsequently throughout the high school years. The administration can do its part by providing a flexible curriculum with a variety of courses designed to challenge both the gifted and the slow student.

5

Sensible Record
Keeping

The Care and Wise Use of the Circular File

After a student has graduated, all he leaves behind, beyond some gum under the auditorium seats, is a printed card on which his teachers, counselors and office clerks have duly marked his passage. This bloodless document, succinct and impersonal though it may be, is nevertheless an important tool for the counselor and for future members of society who may want to evaluate the student for a job, a school or a position of importance in the armed forces. Hardly a week passes that does not find at least one request for information on a graduate—sometimes for a student who was graduated 20 years ago. The counselor who is constantly trying to know his clients well will refer to the record frequently to discover what has happened to his counselee in the past in order to prepare for the future.

This permanent record varies in form and content with each school, but certain information is usually included on all forms. When the pupil reaches high school his permanent record, which is initiated when he enters elementary school, will include the usual vital statistics—name, age, birth date, parents' names, etc. It will contain his academic record, from first grade through junior high school. On it will be recorded the results of all standardized group or individual tests. A medical report will accompany the record. Beyond this, there are a hundred variations. He may have been evaluated on citizenship, leadership, on the socioeconomic level of his home, on his interests, hobbies, his riding habits, or on any one of innumerable and often trivial characteristics. From this last remark you may infer that I have some question in my mind as to what properly belongs in the permanent record. What, indeed, should be permanent?

First of all, a permanent record should include only those items that are useful and significant beyond the immediate grade and age level. Also it should be compact. It takes only a few years to fill an office full of bulky documents, and schools are crowded enough as it is. Finally, since someone has to do the recording and clerical help is always in short supply, there should be a reasonable limit as to how much information is to be recorded. For most schools, a degree of selectivity is advised if the record is expected to be completed.

I'd like to return to the first statement concerning what items of significance should be permanently inscribed. While teachers' comments and personality rating sheets have an immediate value, I question the practice of including these subjective judgments, accurate though they may be, in the permanent record. It seems to me that, in so doing, we are pinning the youngster down at a particular stage of development—apparently assuming he will not change or develop further. Such could not be farther from the actual fact! We see these high school kids at a very trying stage in most cases. Two or three years effects a miraculous change in terms of personality development. To present these youngsters to an eventual employer as they were in high school is grossly unfair. I think this is an invasion of privacy. I have always admired the prose of one of my teaching colleagues who, in the distant past, recorded (in his yearly anecdotal summary) these unforgettable words: "The only thing John passed this term was wind and water." Actually, this summed up poor John very well at the time. He wasn't exactly a winner, but it's just as well that this evaluation was not included in his permanent record. He is now the president of a multimillion dollar corporation.

What should be recorded

The following are suggested items to be included in the record.

A. Vital statistics

    1. Name, address, telephone number, birth date, place of birth.

    2. Names of parents and address if different. It is important to know whether the child is living with both parents, a guardian, or whatever. Seven times out of ten, as a rough estimate, a problem student will have a broken home background. This type of information is not always readily available.

    3. Names and birth dates of brothers and sisters.

    4. Date the pupil entered school and date of leaving with reasons for leaving (moved to_____, withdrew because of scholastic failure, etc.).

    5. Father's occupation, mother's occupation or guardian's occupation.

I don't think socio-economic information should be on the permanent record. This also can be considered an invasion of privacy. It is useful information which the school should know but it shouldn't be permanently recorded—perhaps in anecdotal form appended to the record. This type of information is difficult to obtain and is often a highly subjective judgment based on incomplete observation.

B. The scholastic record from first grade through high school, together with record of attendance. Important: there should be an explanatory notation made on the record in any case of extended absence. Employers are always checking on the attendance records of our graduates. A record of 20 absences in the senior year is understandable if it's the result of an appendix operation. If it's the result of chronic poor health, it isn't a very good recommendation. The lack of a reasonable explanation can hurt a youngster's chances.

C. The testing record, including all subtests scored on multi-factor tests; i.e. verbal, nonverbal and total I.Q. if the California Mental Maturity Test is used, for example.

D. The pupil's offices, honors and activities in high school, part-time jobs, dates, nature of jobs, and names of employers.

E. Post-high school placement and five-year follow-up report.

Such useful information as student interests, autobiographies, teacher evaluations of personality, etc. should be with but not part of the record. We use a folder in our school which houses the actual record and provides a convenient receptable for ratings, etc. These items can be tossed out when the student graduates. We are investigating the possibilities of having all records over ten years old microfilmed for storage purposes.

Obtaining and Recording Information

All this material must be gathered and recorded. As stated above, this is the chief limitation of the amount of material to be included.

The permanent record is ordinarily initiated at registration for kindergarten or first grade. The registration blank will provide the vital statistics available at that time. Any changes are supposed to be reported by homeroom teachers each year from then on. Marks, test results, evaluations, etc. are usually recorded by homeroom teachers until the pupil reaches junior high. Then the work is divided between the counselor and the office staff.

A questionnaire given to freshmen in guidance classes or homerooms can be useful. A sample questionnaire is shown in Figure 3.

Counselors usually have the responsibility of recording test results, activities, placement in colleges and occupations and reports

Figure 3

Student Questionnaire

1. Name ....

              (last)   (first)   (middle)

2. Address ....

          (street and number)   (town)

3. Date of birth .... 4. Age ....

          (month, day, year)   (as of Oct. 1, 19__)

Figure 3 (*cont.*)

5. Place of birth ....

6. Name of father ....

7. His occupation ....

8. His place of employment ....

9. Name of mother ....

10. Her occupation (if other than housewife) ....

11. Her place of employment ....

12. Is any language other than English spoken in your home? ......
    What? ....

13. Can you speak any language other than English? ....
    What? ....

14. Names and ages of brothers and sisters ....

15. Are your facilities for home study good, fair, or poor? ....

16. Do you come to school by bus? ....

17. Are you employed regularly after school, or on Saturdays? ....
    What type of work? .... During what hours? ....

18. Name of employer .... Place of employment ....

19. Did you work during summer vacation? ....
    What type of work did you do? ....
    Name and address of employer ....

20. What occupational field would you like to enter? ....

21. Do you have a second choice? ....

22. Do you plan to continue your education? ....

23. Name of your school chosen, or type of institution ....

24. Have you any favorite school subjects? ...... What? ....

25. What magazines do you read regularly? ....

26. Do you read a newspaper regularly? ....

27. Do you take books from the public library, other than those required for your school work? ...... What type of books do you prefer? ....

28. What are your hobbies? ....

29. Mention any awards you have won in connection with school or your community ....

30. To what clubs, outside of school, do you belong? ....

31. To what school clubs do you belong, or in what school activities are you taking part? ....

32. What sports do you like to play best? ....

33. Who is your family doctor? ....

34. Have you any physical disabilities that would be likely to interfere in any way with your class work or school attendance? ....

from colleges. This is only one reason why full-time clerical help is necessary in the guidance office.

The office staff is responsible for recording marks, attendance, rank in class, etc. In our school, marks are recorded by the subject teachers on rank sheets. Final grades are then transferred to the permanent record by the office staff.

Use of permanent record

Counselors are constantly referring to the permanent record; this is one reason why the records should be located near the guidance office—or vice versa.

We always check the permanent record before and during any major interview with students or parents involving decisions related to the "planned program." I find that, with time, I have memorized a sort of total picture of a student's record by the senior year, but I still need the record to check on details. This should be standard procedure in any guidance program. As a practical note, the record should be made of *durable* material!

If a parent wants to know why Johnny is not performing well in the college course in high school, I pull out the record to see what Johnny's past performance has been. I may find a record of mediocre grades and test results which suggest that the father has overly-ambitious plans for his boy. I then have some facts before me that I can present in arriving at a more realistic program for the boy. If the record shows high scores, we investigate the possible reasons for under-achievement. If the record shows a sudden drop in marks, I ask if Johnny has just received his driver's license, and we go on from there. There are many facts on the record that suggest clues for performance—extended absences (we are not always aware of them even though I try to remember to check the list of absentees daily), poor preparation in preceding courses, lack of effort (as shown by teacher reports which are included in the folder), etc.

INTERVIEW RECORDS

Since counselors usually do not have photographic memories, some method should be developed to keep track of what has been discussed during interviews. I do not believe in lengthy, highly detailed summaries that take 10 or 15 minutes to prepare. They take up too much valuable time and are not necessary. We use notebooks with our counselees listed alphabetically with homeroom and study periods noted—one notebook for each class. After we see pupils, we jot down brief notes summarizing the main points of the discussion. It takes only a few words to refresh your memory. You will be surprised at how much you do recall. We add college board scores and school or job placement choices as these matters are discussed. This has the advantage, also, of insuring that we see all of each class during each phase of the planned program. How much is recorded depends on the individual counselor. The following is a sample page from such an interview record of seniors starting with grade 10. The names have been changed.

Room 105

Long, Jack A5, A7 MWF (Study Halls)

9/25/x4	Orientation. Likes sports—wants college—coaching? Well-adjusted.
1/15/x5	Registration—repeat geometry?
5/10/x5	Will take geometry review in summer.
10/10/x5	Help sessions in Algebra 2 (Mosser). Made varsity.
2/9/x6	Registration. No more math; O.K. by parents.
6/3/x6	S.A.T. V490 M450. Ach. Chem 500. Wants Springfield college. Bridgeport, Holyoke Community? Pitched no hitter vs. Holyoke.
10/14/x6	Applied Springfield, Bridgeport, Holyoke Comm., W.S.C. Wants teacher-coach. Will take writing sample.
2/28/x7	S.A.T. V510 M465. Ach. Eng. 480, MI 450 Help sessions in French 4.
5/15/x7	Accepted Springfield.

Lunt, Mary C3, A7

9/20/x4	Orientation. Blonde bombshell, a little on guard. Business course.

11/17/x4	Already in academic trouble. Call home. Help session in bookkeeping—tutor with Teresa K—3rd period. Goes steady with John Mc!
2/27/x5	Drop biology, parents O.K. Registration—no language.
3/8/x5	How to study. Going steady with Paul A.
6/5/x5	Check on program.
10/15/x5	Skipped school. Trouble at home, conference with parents 10/17/x5.
10/17/x5	Parents' conference. Tough father, easy mother. Advise closer supervision—compromise on nights out.
2/26/x6	Failure notice in typing 2, arrange for help during study 3rd period. Wants office work. Goes steady with Eddie M. Registration.
6/10/x6	Check on program. Advise home management instead of stenography 2.
11/7/x6	Suggest Business school. She wants to go away from home. Greenfield & Berkshire Community. Will take S.A.T.
3/5/x7	S.A.T. V410 M350. Still going with Eddie!
5/15/x7	Accepted on condition by Greenfield—summer course, terminal general business. Halleluiah!

The others on the record are similar. It took less than a minute to write down a few notes after each session. The accumulated record would make little sense to anyone but the counselor, but you can read between the lines. Jack was a hard-working athletic type of all-American boy from a nice family. He was not a strong student, had trouble with geometry, but plugged away. On the field he was outstanding in our football and baseball leagues. He ended up where I think he belongs, in an excellent physical education program.

Mary L. was a filly of a different color. Gorgeous and spoiled at 14, she grew cuter and harder to handle each year. She was understandably interested in the boys, who lost no time reciprocating enthusiastically. She was rebellious at home but was a reasonably good school citizen, although indifferently motivated. We developed a good relationship. She would listen to me, although she didn't always heed my words of wisdom. She finally settled down and did a creditable job in her senior year. Eddie was good for her. I think she'll be O.K.—things are better at home.

Neither record makes any mention of the many times I chatted with either Jack or Mary, of the times I stopped one of them in the corridor to ask a question, or of the numerous quick sessions before school to check briefly on their progress.

THE FOUR-YEAR INDIVIDUAL PROGRAM

I recommend the use of a card, initiated in eighth grade, signed by parents, that shows the four-year program of studies. This is a working record. We refer to it when planning for each succeeding year, making changes, etc. From it the student makes out his registration card. It will show what courses were planned and what changes were made as the student progressed. On it the junior high counselor notes the latest I.Q. score in code. He may clip on anecdotal notes if there is special information he would like to pass on to the high school counselors. We keep these cards on file in our desks along with a copy of the daily program. Following is a sample individual program card.

WESTFIELD HIGH SCHOOL
INDIVIDUAL PROGRAM CARD

NAME: Thomas Hancock   COUNSELOR: S. Adams

Freshman			Sophomore		
	GRADE	POINT		GRADE	POINT
Eng. 1C	C	1	Eng. 2C	D	1
Geog.	C	1	Hist. 2C	D	1
Alg. 1C	E	0	Geom.	D	1
Gen. Sci.	C	1	Bio.	C	1
French 1	D	1	French 2		
Phys. Ed. 1	C	¼	French 1		
		4¼	dropped		0
			Phys. Ed. 2	C	¼
					9½

Summer course—Alg. 1C—C 1

Junior	GRADE	POINT	*Senior*	GRADE	POINT
Eng. 3CG	C	1	Eng. 4CG	C	1
Hist. 3CG	C	1	Prob. CG	B	1
French 3			Chem.		
Alg. 2	D	1	dropped		0
Mech.			Economics	D	1
Draw. 1	B	½	Mech.		
Shop 1	B	½	Draw. 2	B	½
Phys. Ed. 3	B	¼	Shop 2	B	½
		13¾	Phys. Ed. 4	C	¼
					18

Course: College—change to general 3/12/x4
Vocational plans: Lawyer—Machine designer

Signed: *Richard Hancock*

THE FOLLOW-UP STUDY

A record of what happens to one's counselee is always illuminating. It is first an evaluation of the guidance process and the effectiveness of the overall program and, secondly, a convenient record of each graduate that is occasionally referred to during the years. We advise one-year and five-year follow-up studies.

We have already seen how the follow-up can be used in evaluating the guidance program. Some follow-up reports include questions about the curriculum that are intended to sound out graduates as to the strength and weaknesses of the school's program. I am of the opinion that the answers—most of which can be accurately anticipated—are worthless as guidelines for improvement. Most schools are aware of their deficiencies, and whereas we welcome comments from our visiting graduates, the limitations of space on a return follow-up card makes such opinion polls next to worthless. We have tried it with no success. We use a return post card questionnaire, followed up by a letter if necessary. Also, we use the phone when possible, particularly on the one-year follow-up. This is the easy one since you already know what most of your former counselees are doing. One should get close to 100 per cent returns on this. We expect about 75–80 per cent returns on the five-year follow-up. Samples of the studies are shown in Figures 4 and 5.

In addition, we keep an individual list of graduates in the one-year follow-up, showing what they are doing and where they are. The five-year follow-up return card is tossed into the permanent record folder—a convenient receptacle for anything we don't know what to do with. But sometimes we do find a use for these reports. Some employer may be looking for a boy just out of the service, etc.

The five-year report reveals some interesting data concerning our graduates. We find, for instance, that over 75 per cent of the girls are married within five years of graduation. Only 25 per cent of the boys are married. I'd like to think that this is

Figure 4

FIVE-YEAR FOLLOW-UP—CLASS OF 1960
(As of June, 1967)

Total number of graduates—288
Total number of direct returns—152 (89 girls; 63 boys)
Total number about whom some information was obtained by phone calls, or other indirect contacts.
    —111 (65 girls; 46 boys)

Total number of returns (4 boys deceased)	263	(91%)
No information obtained	25	(9%)
Total members in class	288	

AT SCHOOL	Boys	Girls
Presently working for doctorate	3	2
Presently attending 4-year colleges	11	0
Presently attending graduate school	7	4
Presently attending other schools:		
Junior College	1	0
IBM or Data Processing	0	1
LPN School	0	1
Total	22	8

—   30 or 11%

Figure 4 *(cont.)*

COMPLETED	Boys	Girls
4-Year Colleges	52	26
Graduate School	8	8
2-Year Business Schools	5	6
2-Year Junior College	5	2
Nursing:		
Hospital RN		12
Pract. Nurse School		4
Child Care		1
2-Year Tech. Schools	5	
Special Schools:	8	22
Including Dental Asst., Hairdresser, Art, Design, IBM, Comptometer, Barber School, Banking, and Photography Schools.		
Total	83	81

— 164 or 62%

AT WORK	Boys	Girls
Clerical	7	25
Teaching	15	13
Engineering	16	0
Nursing: R.N.'s	0	8
L.P.N.'s	0	2
Beauticians and Barbers	2	9
Retail	2	3
Sales	9	2
Others—Including 1 boy and 2 girls who are serving or have served in the Peace Corps.	21	12
Total	72	74

— 146 or 56%

ARMED FORCES	Boys	Girls
Presently serving	28	0
Completed service	18	0
Total	46	0

— 46 or 17%

	Boys	Girls
MARRIED	44 (17%)	126 (48%)
HOUSEWIVES		46 (17%)
UNEMPLOYED		2 (8%)

Percentage for *all* but the number reporting is computed on the number of returns, *263*, not on the original class size, *288*.

Figure 5

Westfield High School

FOLLOW-UP STUDY
CLASS OF 1964

	Girls—189 Boys—129 Total—318	
At School	No.	% of Class
Colleges & Universities—4 yr.	110	35%
Junior Colleges	24	
Nursing Schools	21	
Business Schools	23	
Technical Schools	7	
Preparatory Schools	5	
Miscellaneous Schools	22	
	212	66%
At Work		
Agriculture	2	
Clerical	38	
Manufacturing	13	
Retail Trade	15	
	68	21%
Armed Forces		
Army	3	
Navy	4	
Air Force	8	
Marines	1	
	16	6%
Unemployed	13	4%
Married	7	2%
No Returns	2	1%

evidence that men are smarter than women, but I'm afraid it's more likely due to the relative immaturity of boys and the fact that they have more to do in order to qualify for connubial bliss— further education, service obligation, developing financial security, etc.

We also find another 10 or 15 per cent of the class who entered college or school after work or the service. These include many "hopeless" individuals who were the despair of their parents and the hairshirts of the faculty.

We find out what students left college before graduation, although we are usually not given the reasons. We see how many graduates are still working in their chosen field—how many have changed. This gives us a *rough* evaluation of our counseling effectiveness. Of course, the report does not tell us the important facts: How well are our graduates handling the problems of life? Are they happy? Are they contributing to society? Have they made the most of their potential? These things we can only guess at as we read between the lines.

ANECDOTAL RECORDS

From time to time, teachers and counselors from the lower grades turn up some significant information that should be passed along to others via the permanent record—not as part of it but along with it.

Counselors in the high school appreciate such advance information which can be relayed to teachers if necessary. Such things as physical defects appear on the medical record, but are apt to be missed. We'd like to know who has defective sight or hearing—and so do the faculty. I recently discovered a boy who had a glass eye and nobody knew it until December of his senior year! It was on the record and the nurse assumed we were aware of the problem. In this case, the boy didn't seem to have suffered academically—but still we should have known. We now make a point of circulating lists of students with significant physical defects to teachers—lists compiled by the school nurse at the start of each year.

We are often advised to expect problems in cases of rebellious youngsters, kids from difficult family situations, broken homes, recent deaths, etc., by means of anecdotal notes from the junior high counselors. This is invaluable information.

This kind of communication between schools and faculty—or within a school—by the use of informal anecdotal reports is obviously a very desirable practice.

Our vice-principal works very closely with the guidance department, and we always get a copy of any letters sent home to parents in cases of more extreme disciplinary actions. This also is a great help in keeping the counselor informed.

FAILURE NOTICES

We try to keep parents informed as to their children's progress. Of course, report cards are sent home at the end of each marking period. In addition, teachers make reports of failures or near failures at mid-term. These are sent home by the office. We have no way of knowing how many are intercepted by alert and apprehensive students, but we retain a copy and a copy goes in the student's permanent record folder. This report, at least, alerts the pupil, his family and his counselor.

Conclusion

Because much of the material used by the teacher and counselor is useful only while the pupil is in school, it is advisable to use some sort of folder that can house this information temporarily, information to be discarded after it has fulfilled its use. I think it important to avoid setting up a *permanent* judgment of a youngster who has not "jelled."

Some of the record forms I have suggested as being useful in the counselor's work are illustrated in Figures 6, 7, 8, and 9. Note that Figure 7 represents older forms and the various parts of Figure 8 the newer, streamlined versions. Figure 9, the Cumulative Record, doubles as a file envelope in which the student's records can be kept. It is up to the individual counselor to change these to his particular needs or to add other forms. As a general rule, however, I advise against voluminous and unnecessarily detailed record keeping. Pare it down to essentials. Time is precious in the guidance department, and frequent use of the waste basket will prevent an accumulation of useless or prejudicial junk.

I suggest the following reference for those who wish more detailed information—particularly on the permanent record: Arthur E. Traxler, *Techniques of Guidance* (Evanston, Illinois: Harper and Row, 1966).

PHILLIPS
LI
PROVIDE

SCHOOL — INDIVIDUAL PLAN

Class.......... Counselor..........

...........s Beyond High School.......... ....
....
Curriculum.......... ....

FIRST YEAR	SECOND YEAR	THIRD YEAR	FOURTH YEAR

The above program has been planned with my approval, and no changes are to be made either in the objectives of the plan or in its details without written authority except as may seem necessary to school officials.

Date.......... ....Parent or Guardian

Figure 6

MEMORIAL
RARY
NCE COLLEGE

C

SOCIAL AND PERSONAL RECORD

_____ PUBLIC SCHOOLS

_____, MASSACHUSETTS

1. NAME _____

LAST   FIRST   MIDDLE

2. DATE OF BIRTH _____

YEAR   MONTH   DAY

3. FAMILY HISTORY

FATHER LIVING _____ MOTHER LIVING _____ LIVES WITH BOTH _____ IF NOT, WHICH ONE ? _____

IF NOT LIVING WITH PARENTS, LIVES WITH _____ RELATION, IF ANY ?

4.	NAME	ADDRESS	PLACE OF BIRTH—CITY, STATE, ETC.	OTHER PERTINENT INFORMATION
COMPLETE FOR	MOTHER			
PARENTS OR	FATHER			
PEOPLE WITH				
WHOM LIVING				

5.	FATHER'S OCCUPATION	EMPLOYER	DATE	REMARKS	MOTHER'S OCCUPATION	EMPLOYER	DATE	REMARKS

6.	BROTHERS AND SISTERS IN ORDER OF AGE	DATE OF BIRTH	OCCUPATION (IF WORKING)	REMARKS
OTHER MEMBERS OF FAMILY				

Figure 7A

13 ACTIVITIES, INTEREST AND NEEDS

GRADE	GRADE	GRADE

14 VOCATIONAL EXPERIENCES DURING SCHOOL YEARS

DATE	KIND OF WORK	EMPLOYER	DATES FROM–TO	HOURS PER WK.	WAGES PER WK.	LIKED JOBS YES	LIKED JOBS NO

15 VOCATIONAL INTEREST TESTS

DATE	TEST	FINDINGS

16 EDUCATION BEYOND PUBLIC SCHOOL

DATES	INSTITUTION	REMARKS

17 EMPLOYMENT AFTER LEAVING SCHOOL

DATES FROM–TO	EMPLOYER	POSITION

Figure 7A (cont.)

SCHOLASTIC RECORD, Grades K-8

PUBLIC SCHOOLS
MASSACHUSETTS

1 NAME ___ LAST ___ FIRST ___ MIDDLE

2 DATE OF BIRTH ___ MONTH ___ DAY ___ YEAR

3

4

5

GRADE	DATE ENT'RED	DATE M.D.AAA	AGE OCT. I	DAYS ABSENT	DAYS P'ES'NT	TIMES TARDY	TIMES D'MS'D	SCHOOL	TEACHER	READING	LAN. GUAGE	PENMAN-SHIP	SPELL-ING	ARITH-METIC	SOCIAL STUDIES	SCI-ENCE	MUSIC	ART	HEALTH &PH.ED.	PROM'D 1/ G#2/

ABILITY AND ACHIEVEMENT TEST RECORD, Grades K-8

MENTAL ABILITY TESTS

6

DATE	GRADE	TEST USED	C.A.	M.A.	I.Q.

ACHIEVEMENT TESTS

7

DATE	GRADE	SUBJECT	TEST USED	C.A.	E.A.	GRADE P'EN'T

ACHIEVEMENT TESTS

7-CONT.

DATE	GRADE	TEST USED	SUBJECT	C.A.	E.A.	GRADE P'EN'T

Figure 7B

B

SCHOLASTIC RECORD, Grades 9-12

8 NAME _____ LAST _____ FIRST _____ MIDDLE _____ **9 DATE OF BIRTH** _____ YEAR, MONTH, DAY _____ **10 ENTERED** _____ DATE _____ **11 FROM** _____ SCHOOL OR CITY

12

YEAR	GRADE	MK.	CR.	YEAR	GRADE	MK	CR.	YEAR	GRADE	MK.	CR.	YEAR	GRADE	MK.	CR.

PER. LENGTH		TOTAL		PER. LENGTH		TOTAL		PER. LENGTH		TOTAL		PER. LENGTH		TOTAL	
ABS.	TARDY	DISM.		ABS.	TARDY	DISM.		ABS.	TARDY	DISM.		ABS.	TARDY	DISM.	

ABILITY AND ACHIEVEMENT TEST RECORD, Grades 9-12

13 MENTAL ABILITY TESTS

DATE	GRADE	TEST USED	C.A.	M.A.	I.Q.

14 ACHIEVEMENT TESTS

DATE	GRADE	TEST USED	SUBJECT	C.A.	E.A.	GRAD. PLAC.

15

DATE	LEFT OR REENTERED	REASON FOR LEAVING

16 REMARKS

GRADUATED ON _____

RANK _____ NO. IN CLASS _____

CREDITS SENT TO _____

Figure 7B (cont.)

PERSONAL RECORD

_____ PUBLIC SCHOOLS

_____, MASS.

NAME _____ LAST _____ FIRST _____ MIDDLE

DATE OF BIRTH _____

YEAR   MONTH   DAY

FATHER LIVING   MOTHER LIVING   LIVES WITH BOTH   IF NOT, WHICH ONE ?

IF NOT LIVING WITH PARENTS, LIVES WITH   RELATION, IF ANY ?

COMPLETE FOR PARENTS OR PEOPLE WITH WHOM LIVING	NAME	ADDRESS	BIRTH PLACE, CITY, STATE	MOTHER'S MAIDEN NAME	OTHER INFORMATION
	MOTHER				
	FATHER				

FATHER'S OCCUPATION	EMPLOYER	REMARKS	MOTHER'S OCCUPATION	EMPLOYER	REMARKS

BROTHERS AND SISTERS IN ORDER OF AGE | DATE OF BIRTH

PHOTOGRAPHS:

REMARKS :

Figure 8A

SCHOLASTIC RECORD

GRADES K-8

_____ PUBLIC SCHOOLS
_____, MASS.

NAME _____
LAST   FIRST   MIDDLE

DATE OF BIRTH _____
YEAR   MONTH   DAY

GRADE	DATE ENTER	DATE W'DRWN	AGE OCT. I	DAYS ABSENT	DAYS P'ENT	TIMES TARDY	TIMES D'MISD	SCHOOL	TEACHER	READING VOC	READING UNDER STDNG	LANGUAGE ORAL	LANGUAGE WRIT-TEN	SPELLING TESTS	SPELLING OTHER	ARITHMETIC COMP	ARITHMETIC PROB	WRITING	SCI	SOC. ST.	MUSIC	ART	HEALTH

TEST RECORDS

MENTAL ABILITY TESTS

DATE	GRADE	TEST	I. Q

ACHIEVEMENT TESTS

GRADES K-8

Figure 8B-1

_____ HIGH SCHOOL   **SCHOLASTIC RECORD**   GRADES 9-12

_____, MASS.

NAME _____   DATE OF BIRTH _____   ENTERED _____ DATE _____ FROM _____
       LAST   FIRST   MIDDLE   YEAR MONTH DAY   SCHOOL OR CITY

YEAR	GRADE	MK	CR									
TOTAL												
ABS. TARDY DISM.												

TEST RECORD

RANK IN CLASS _____ NO. IN CLASS _____ BASED ON PERIOD FROM _____ TO _____ GRADUATED –

CREDITS SENT TO	SCHOOL OR JOB PLACEMENT	DATE	LEFT OR REENTERED

93-100A, 85-92B, 77-84C 70-76D   PRINCIPAL _____
BELOW 70, FAILURE

Figure 8B-2

1. NAME_____

LAST   FIRST   MIDDLE

2. BIRTH_____

MONTH DAY YEAR   CITY   STATE

3. SEX_____

5. VACCINATED_____

6. AUTHORITY FOR BIRTH DATE_____

CUMULATIVE RECORD

_____ PUBLIC SCHOOLS

MASSACHUSETTS

A

7

B

DATE	HOME ADDRESS	TEL. NO.	SCHOOL	GRADE	TEACHER	TRANSFERRED TO	DATE	SIGNATURE OF PRINCIPAL

Figure 9

6

School and College

Placement

Multiple Applications and Aspirin

Spring is a time when a young man's fancy turns to thoughts of college admission. Romance takes a back seat in March and April as our young candidates exist on a diet of aspirin and fingernails. For the counselor, college admissions is an important activity, as well as school admission for the noncollege student. We probably spend the greater part of our time counseling on school and college choice—particularly with juniors and seniors. I have already stated that my goal—which will obviously never be reached—is to send *all* of our students who can benefit from further education on to school after graduation. This is a good, solid, practical goal and, although it does not sound as impressive as "self-fulfillment," "self-actualization," and other more noble purposes of the guidance experts, it is a goal that is attainable and may well serve as an important step toward developing a youngster's ability to cope successfully with the problems of life. This is one area where the counselor's knowledge and experience is put to its most effective use. School and college placement, by itself, would justify the existence of a guidance program in most schools.

Let's pursue the idea of post-high school training for all. Is it a legitimate goal? One need only look around at the world of work to be immediately impressed by the importance of further education for all. The classified ads are full of requests for highly-trained and skilled workers—draftsmen, designers, tool makers, and technicians of all types. One sees few requests for truck drivers or elevator operators. It's the IBM experts, not just typists, that are in demand. This need for trained specialists is reflected in a variety of ways. Salesmen are given lengthy and expensive training programs. Businesses are sending their bookkeepers to night school in college courses of accounting and are paying the bills. Industries have developed all manner of in-service training programs.

The demand for further training by society has resulted in an explosion of two-year junior colleges—public and private—which offer terminal courses in technical, paramedical and business skills, in addition to the regular college transfer course. The current tendency is to lengthen the educational experience for all—both in the areas of the liberal arts and in technical, vocational courses.

There is another reason why I emphasize school placement. It has a lot to do with occupational choice. We will see in a later chapter that occupational counseling is a difficult process. Despite courses in occupations and hours of counseling, most high school graduates take *whatever jobs are available*—not those for which they might be best fitted. It is easier to get a student interested in a particular kind of school than in a particular job. Obviously, there must be some sort of prior occupational choice involved in the selection of the school. But the opportunity to enter a particular job field is much better if the youngster graduates from an advanced school. It is, in a sense, a kind of guarantee that he will be placed in his field. Unfortunately, not all students will want to—or be able to—go on to further schooling. These will end up as clerks, bench workers, packers, etc. It is true that a larger percentage of workers are in this type of unskilled work, but the opportunities are not there and, to escape this category of work, further training is necessary.

It seems obvious to me—as it does to many others in education, industry and the professions—that since we are living in a period of civilization when technology and science are developing in all directions with dizzying speed, we need more and more trained people in all walks of life to keep pace with this change, to control it and to profit from it. I don't mean to imply that all our kids should be scientists or technicians. On the contrary, we need philosophers and humanitarians even more if the world is to survive. This is an extremely unoriginal idea, but it bears repetition.

But whether they be physicists, philosophers or electronic technicians, we need trained and educated people. This is where the counselor steps into the picture. I have seen few students in high school who could not benefit from some kind of post-high school training. Our task is to insure that each pupil is encouraged to reach the limit of his potential.

What schools for whom?

Relatively few pupils and their parents are fully aware of the educational opportunities available—or the requirements of these various schools. However, the counselor knows—or should find out. I have also discovered that parents and students generally are receptive to the idea of further education. The parents are thinking in terms of financial security; the students are eager to learn—or willing to postpone the inevitable entry into the adult world. There is also a tremendous national awareness of the importance of education at this time as we all know. So, if you're located near centers of education, it's relatively easy to get kids interested in schools. Once the counselor has pointed out the possibilities, most parents are enthusiastic. Then it comes down to the matter of what school for what youngster.

At the risk of over-generalization, the following are some brief sketches intended to characterize the qualified candidate for a number of categories of schools and colleges.

1. THE LIBERAL ARTS COLLEGE

The youngster who has the best chance to benefit from a liberal arts college will usually be in the top quarter of his class in a general high school, with an average grade of B or better in a college course. He will usually have an I.Q. of 115 or higher, read about the 60%tile and possess good *verbal* ability. He will have a measure of self-discipline, maturity, and hopefully, curiosity. I would prefer him to be a little naive and wide-eyed rather than a sophisticated know-it-all. He should be reasonably independent and self-directed. He will be happier if he has developed some extra-curricular interests, such as athletics, music, dramatics, school publications and the like. And he should like people. Quite a paragon? Not really, if you judge students in relation to their peers—not by adult standards. Remember, they will develop.

I know there are many with lower I.Q.'s or poorer grades who are college material and who will go on to prove it. This is an *ideal* candidate we're picturing.

2. Engineering Colleges

This student should have most of the same qualifications as the liberal arts candidate, but his strength should lie in mathematics and science. I feel that—as a rule of thumb—a candidate should score at least 600 in the Math SAT score to be qualified for a good engineering school. In addition, he should be interested in practical things—in the *application* of ideas, not in ideas for their own sake. He should be able to push himself, have confidence in himself and be capable of an aggressive approach to problems. After all, this boy will soon be in the competitive world of industry. He must also be more sure of his vocational goal since he has less opportunity to change in the specialized engineering school.

About one in five of the graduates from our school that enter engineering eventually transfer into either liberal arts or business administration. I'm not saying this is bad—it's only a fact and it points out the rather exacting qualifications required of the engineering candidate. In these cases, I anticipate about half the transfers on the basis of personality traits. They were thinkers rather than doers.

Part of the attraction of engineering for these students, I believe, rests in the fact that mathematics and science have far more appeal in high school than do the humanities. I suspect it is a matter of maturity. They're usually not old enough to appreciate the possibilities in the humanities. In any case, if a boy is undecided between engineering and liberal arts, I think he would be wise to choose liberal arts, which is less specialized and leads in more directions. This, despite the fact that it is easier for a qualified applicant to get into engineering schools where there is still a lack of good candidates.

3. BUSINESS ADMINISTRATION COLLEGES

In general, I find that business administration colleges do not require as much verbal ability as do the liberal arts and engineering schools. A student should have taken the college course, although he might have substituted some business courses for the language and taken a lighter dose of math or science. He should be methodical, accurate and practical. This does not mean he should lack imagination. He should be a good manager, a planner, well organized. It also helps if his father is chairman of the board.

4. THE TEACHER'S COLLEGE

Assuming the candidate to be a good student in a solid college course, I would expect him to be a person who, above all else, likes people. He should be outgoing, highly verbal, good-humored and honestly concerned with others. We have seen many introverts grow into successful teachers, but I don't think they enjoy it as much as the exuberant extroverts. The problem here is that you don't know how a youngster will develop during college. I have watched so many shy boys and girls develop surprising self-confidence in those four short years!

5. U.S. SERVICE ACADEMIES

This candidate is something out of the ordinary. He *has* to be to survive the rigorous physical and mental discipline demanded. He is emotionally stable, self-confident, aggressive, mature, physically fit and loves a challenge. He is a good student, strong in math and science. He is highly organized and self-disciplined. He has obvious leadership potential. He is indeed a rare bird in most schools!

It is obvious that everyone cannot and should not go to college. I have indicated typical qualifications of the average candidates for the average college. However, there are all kinds of colleges, and the students who could not qualify for one might be successful in another less demanding college. Some of our academically "hopeless" graduates who spent four years in the service are surprising us all by their success in good schools. Maturity and purpose make such a difference.

There is a scholastic limit below which a student's chances seem remote. In these cases, the counselor has a responsibility to inform the student and the parent of his estimate of the situation—and the earlier the better. I try to offer a substitute plan, such as a two-year school with the possibility of going on later to the degree course. It's much better to be a good electronic technician than a poor electrical engineer. And there are so many opportunities that lead to interesting, rewarding occupations. Armed with this information, the counselor has a better chance to make his point. Of course, much of the choice is made by the admissions boards of most colleges who will discourage the obviously limited student. But we should help our counselees avoid the bitter experience of being rejected. As one of my students exclaimed with stars in her eyes, "It's so nice that somebody wants me!" Again I remind the reader that because of our location, most of our kids apply to schools in highly competitive New England. The game of college admissions can be a grim business for some kids pushed by well-meaning but unrealistic parents.

This is a good point at which to emphasize what is becoming increasingly apparent to us rock-bound New Englanders. We can be justifiably proud of our fine institutions, but we would be blindly insular not to admit that other parts of the country have excellent schools as well. Counselors, educators and students all bring back enthusiastic reports of schools from beyond the borders. It becomes increasingly imperative that the counselor constantly expand his contacts with the knowledge of schools outside his area. I'm a great believer in the educational values of going away from home to school—to meet people from different parts of the country, to visit different areas, to get away from the family. It has a maturing influence on the student and a sedative effect on the parents.

6. NURSE'S TRAINING

This girl, like the teacher candidate, likes people, is concerned for others, and is dedicated to a career of service. She is practical, dependable, works well with people, does not flinch from hard work and has a toughness of fibre that will see her through the trying moments that are a part of every nurse's daily routine. To qualify for a college degree, she must be an excellent student (in many colleges, the school of nursing is more selective than the liberal arts school). These days, R.N. training is also quite selective and demands above average grades, while the practical nurse's course has become likewise more competitive. The reason is a growing demand for nurses coupled with a slow growth in training facilities. Also, the advance of medical science requires more intelligent, highly trained nurses.

7. JUNIOR COLLEGES

These two-year schools offer such a variety of programs that it is difficult to generalize. They usually offer a transfer course into a four-year college, as well as terminal courses. In the case of the former, the candidate will have satisfied the course requirements required by the four-year college that the student intends to enter eventually. This student is often a "late bloomer," has potential but hasn't achieved up to capacity. He is immature but shows signs of purpose and wants to go on to college. If a girl, she may be unsure of her goals, is unwilling to commit herself to four years of study. Perhaps both the girl and boy want the specialized training offered by the terminal courses—business, technology or medical services.

The growth of the state community colleges has put this type of education within the financial reach of thousands of students. In our area, the state community college has been a lifesaver. It will take our under-achievers with potential and give them a chance to prove themselves. We're always delighted at the high percentage of these academic risks who measure up to the demands of the rigorous transfer course. These colleges are expanding their offerings of terminal courses, as well. The growth of the community college has been a very significant and welcome development that has taken place during the past five years in our state and throughout the East.

8. TECHNICAL SCHOOLS

Sometimes part of the community college, sometimes an independent and separate school, the technical school is finally getting the recognition it deserves. It supplies industry with its sorely needed technicians, engineering assistants, and highly trained specialists.

The typical candidate will have taken two, preferably three, years of college math plus science. He will like mechanical drawing, working with gadgets, and building things with his hands. In a way, he will be comparable to the engineering candidate, but at a lower level of scholastic ability.

Since many graduates of technical schools go on eventually to engineering colleges, it is sometimes a convenient entry into this field for the developing under-achiever who would be questionable college material as a senior in high school.

9. BUSINESS SCHOOLS

This candidate will have demonstrated interest and proficiency in the business courses in high school, but wants to develop further skills or specialize in an area such as legal secretary or accounting. If a candidate has taken a college course, it is possible to transfer to a college of business administration, and thus the two-year business school also provides a means of entry into a degree granting course of business administration. Such a candidate has demonstrated potential but has not achieved well enough to warrant direct application to college.

Even though most of our business course graduates can gain immediate employment, I encourage them to go on to further training in business schools. This results in better job security and better placement.

10. TRADE SCHOOL

This candidate is limited in his ability to do scholastic work but possesses skill in the manual and mechanical areas. He wants to specialize in a trade and has taken the general course in high school. We are fortunate in our town to have an excellent trade school that will accept post-graduates on a one- or two-year basis. This offers the student the opportunity of four years of "liberal arts" training in high school as well as specialized training in a trade. In many ways, I believe this is a better educational experience than entering trade school directly—even though it takes longer. After all—what's the hurry?

11. MISCELLANEOUS SCHOOLS

There are numerous schools which offer a variety of specialized training—comptometer, hairdressing, schools for chefs, radio and TV repair, etc. Many state colleges offer two-year programs in agriculture such as horticulture, landscaping, turf maintenance, park management, etc. Many of the general course students will be interested in these schools if they are aware of the opportunities. Qualifications for most of these schools vary, but many will take any high school graduate who is interested and willing to work.

Accumulating a knowledge of educational opportunities

One of the first tasks of the new counselor is to familiarize himself with the educational opportunities in and outside his area. I recommend Lovejoy's *Guide to Colleges* and *Guide to Vocational Schools* as valuable sources of information. There are many such publications available to the counselor.

In addition, a guidance office should have a complete library of college and school catalogs. It is a good idea to have a "career corner" in the school library where duplicate copies of catalogs are located along with source information such as Lovejoy, *The College Blue Book,* and others. A checkout system should be employed by both the guidance office and the library so that these catalogs may be available to students for overnight use.

It takes time to acquire a knowledge of schools, but it is worth it. Most schools welcome visits by touring college admissions officers. We had over sixty such visits last year and find them most helpful in keeping up to date on recent developments and in building a good working relationship with colleges. They are also an inexhaustible source of latest stories.

The purpose of these visits is to provide an opportunity for the admissions representatives to inform students about their respective schools. This can be an important factor in influencing school choice. The students have a chance to ask questions, receive realistic information about entrance standards, and are better able to evaluate the school and their chances of acceptance. It gives the counselor a chance to have the admissions officer glance over records and offer a preliminary evaluation.

I believe that some sort of screening is advisable to limit the attendance at these sessions to those who are reasonably good candidates and who are, or might be, interested in the type of school represented. We post the weekly schedules of the visits and request that the students sign up in advance. We allow the students to miss classes—with teacher approval—to attend the interviews.

More and more school systems are sending the counselors to visit schools outside the immediate area. For those of us within the area of competitive New England colleges, this is a most helpful policy. We ordinarily learn about schools by way of the returning graduate and how he and the school get along together. First hand information is better and increases one's contacts.

However it is done, it is vital to the success of the school placement function that the counselor know schools and be able to suggest those schools for which the youngster best qualifies by reason of ability, interest and personality. He must be able to fit the school and the youngster together in happy accord.

You notice I imply that the counselor takes the initiative for school selection. This is often the case. If the student and his parents are ignorant of school opportunities, it is up to the counselor to suggest possibilities. If the student brings in choices, it is up to the counselor to evaluate them in the light of the student and advise accordingly.

Education vs. training

I'm afraid I'm an incurable optimist. I always know that Lassie will get home and sooner or later Charlie Brown will get a home run. I also believe that humanity will survive and even improve. So it's not surprising that I believe in the value of education—I mean education as opposed to training. I believe that there is such a thing as liberal arts education and that it can be found in many colleges, although the demands of a materialistic society have diluted the quality of education in many institutions. I feel that the ability to think clearly, to communicate fluently and to choose wisely is valuable preparation for life. I think that it is good to expand one's interests, to become involved with the problems of mankind. I would like to see a young person's values based on an appreciation of beauty and excellence in any form. I believe that the liberal arts college will do this for the student who is ready to see and willing to learn. I am convinced that this kind of education—however inadequately I have described it—is better than learning how to earn a living.

Much of the curriculum at any university has become concerned with training—nursing, science, engineering, business administration, etc. I am not about to launch a critique on what a college should be, but there are schools and divisions within schools where a student is first *educated* and training for a career is secondary. This all leads up to the question of who should go to the liberal arts college, and also to the more important question—*does he know why he is going?*

We have already seen that the candidate who will benefit most from a liberal arts college has certain qualifications. He will be highly verbal, interested in abstract ideas and eager to learn. He will be more concerned with the problems of mankind, than in making a fast buck. If he is not, he belongs in a training course. He is not ready to be educated.

He will also be conscious of the purpose of his education. He will be looking for the fruits of learning. He will be receptive to new ideas and experiences. Why will he know and do this? Because his counselor will tell him.

One way or another it is up to the school to sell the idea of education. It is a rare parent that gives more than lip service to education. What they are really thinking about is training—earning a living—job security. This is only natural when you consider that a parent can easily invest $12,000 in his child's college career. So some indoctrination is necessary if a youngster is to approach his college experience with a perceptive mind. If all he looks for is training for a career, he has been cheated out of the real value in his college experience.

While I believe that all youngsters have unique virtues and value them equally, I feel we should do everything we can to encourage the potential liberal arts candidate and prepare him for an exciting, illuminating experience. These are the young men and women who will find the answers to mankind's ills—if anybody can.

I hope I haven't overstated the case for liberal arts and liberal arts candidates. I don't mean to imply that only those who have had this experience can have an influence on the mind and actions of society. We all know better than that. But this is the group that will comprise our thinkers, our poets and philosophers, our future Thomas Paines and Charles Darwins. We are going to *need* these kids, every one of them!

School and college admissions

In a less philosophical vein, let's discuss the more practical aspects of college admissions. College choice is a confusing business, in itself. How to pick a college out of the hundreds of possibilities? There are certain limiting factors that will automatically eliminate certain schools. The student's academic record and the "Board" (or ACT) scores may not be high enough to qualify him for the more selective schools. The costs of some colleges are prohibitive for other students (unless they are good scholarship candidates). Some may want a coeducational institution, or a men's or women's college. There are small colleges where the less aggressive student will be more apt to develop and large universities which will provide a challenge to the self-confident youngsters. There are city colleges and country colleges. And there are colleges that offer special courses such as marine biology, Latin American culture or astronomy. Any of these factors—or merely geographical location—may influence the candidate in his choice of school.

Criteria for College Admission

Colleges vary in their entrance standards, but in all colleges the academic record is by far the most important criterion of selection. High CEEB scores usually will not rescue a student with an unsatisfactory rank in class. However, as pointed out in a previous chapter, the CEEB tests and ACT tests *are* significant factors. The personal qualities of the student and his activities in and out of school will influence the admission board's selection. Finally, the counselor's recommendation is carefully considered.

A brief word concerning recommendations to college. Although it is still termed the "principal's recommendation," guidance counselors are the ones who commonly write the report. We spend hour upon hour in writing these, and it becomes a combined exercise in English "A" (well known by any college freshman) and will power. It taxes the counselor's ability to write four lines of deathless prose (you seldom have room for more on many forms) and his determination not to fall into repetitious and meaningless superlatives. But admissions offices appreciate a perceptive, factual characterization that informs. They don't want an accolade—they would like specific, factual information. It is most important that we present as fair and accurate a picture of the candidate as possible. This is the way to build good rapport with colleges. Most important, we have an obligation to both the student and the school. If the student has a significant weakness, we should spell it out. If he is an insufferable brat, we should say so— but more gracefully. Let the college do the evaluation. At the same time, let's not let our personal prejudices blind us to the potential of these youngsters. An impersonal analysis—factual, descriptive, accurate—is what we should present. It's worth the time and effort. If the candidate warrants it, enclose a whole page, but brevity is the charitable approach. Those poor guys in the admissions office read thousands of these.

In addition to the principal's report, many applications contain a Personality Rating Sheet on which teachers rate the candidate on attitude, effort, and other qualities. We anticipate this by circulating a similar form to the student's teachers late in the junior year. We then have the information in the fall when applications are filled out.

There is a group of selective colleges who enjoy a well-deserved prestige. These schools are looking for honor students, with high board scores, the cream of the crop. At the other end of the scale is a small, rapidly disappearing group of schools who will accept anyone whose body temperature is within two degrees of 98.6° F. In the middle is a large number of excellent schools who are looking for the good, average candidate in the upper third or quarter of his class with board scores in the 500's. These are the schools to cultivate since these are the schools that a large majority of our students will attend. I recommend the *Manual of Freshman Class Profiles* published by the Educational Testing Service as a guide to the degree of selectivity of various colleges. This volume includes tables showing the grades, board scores and other characteristics of the students who applied and of those who were accepted. It gives one a rough picture of the admissions policy of each school.

After preliminary college selections have been made, or even before, it is important that the student visit the campuses of the schools in which he is interested, if at all possible. In our school, we give the students the privilege of missing a day or two of school for this purpose, providing his teachers approve and he is accompanied by an adult. It is only common sense for a student to at least see the campus on which he may spend the next four years. If he can have a session with the admissions officer and attend classes, so much the better.

The candidate should also read the college catalog carefully, noting admission requirements, costs, course offerings and courses required for the degree, extra-curricular activities, special programs and the like. We urge our students to apply to at least three schools and to include an "insurance school." This is a college which we are reasonably certain will accept the candidate and one that he would like to attend although it might not be included in his top choices. This is because even the best students today cannot be sure of acceptance by the school of their choice if they are applying to highly selective schools. Until the supply catches up with the demand, we must all accept the fact that multiple applications are necessary.

Once the choice has been made, the machinery of application can begin. The student will write for an application. This is usually filled out and sent in with the student's academic record and counselor's recommendation at the end of the first marking period, unless the college specifies a different date. Some colleges use an application with personal information to be completed by the student and sent in directly. They then send a second form to the high school for the transcript of grades and recommendations. Most schools will want mid-year grades as well and will not take action on an application until these grades and the college board exams are received. The process of initiating the application is the student's responsibility—as is the whole business of college admission—but the counselor has to do some timely prodding. Make a point of checking on the progress of your counselees.

College boards should be taken in December or January at the latest, the ACT early in the year. Students who plan to take achievement tests should inform the subject teacher. They may have some ideas and suggestions. Candidates should have completed their applications by January. Many colleges close applications in March—some earlier. And whereas others accept students well into the summer, there's no point in waiting longer except in unusual circumstances.

Colleges vary in their policy of accepting candidates. Some use a rolling admissions policy by which they accept the qualified student as soon as the application and board scores are received. Others use the Candidate's Reply Date. Under this system, students are notified of acceptance or rejection in the middle of April. They in turn must inform the college by the reply date (around May 1) whether or not they will attend. Some schools hold out a faint hope by putting marginal students on a waiting list. Rolling admissions holds some hazards for the applicant. He may receive an acceptance early in March, but be waiting to hear from his first choice college which uses the Candidate's Reply Date. Since he usually has to send an enrollment fee of $100 or so within 30 days to hold his place in the college which has already accepted him, it can become an expensive proposition. He is between the Scylla of accepting a sure thing and paying the $100, and the Charybdis of taking a chance on the other. There is often nothing that can be done in this common situation. Sometimes, a telephone call to the admissions director of the first choice college can shed some light on the boy's chances, although the director can't commit himself definitely.

Early Admission: Some colleges will accept outstanding students at the end of their junior year if they have demonstrated unusual academic ability and maturity. These students comprise a very small percentage of those admitted to college and for obvious reasons. I advise counselors and parents to examine the total picture very carefully before encouraging a student to take this step. Many college students lack the maturity to benefit completely from their college experience under a normal admissions time table. Indeed, many students would benefit from a year of work or the service before entering college if the circumstances were favorable.

Early Decision: This is a horse of a different color. In an attempt to take the pressure off the highly qualified applicant, many colleges offer the option of an early decision as to acceptance. While policies vary, the general plan is to accept the application of students in the fall of their senior year if the candidate's overall qualifications are high and if he will promise to attend the college if accepted. Usually, he cannot make applications to other schools unless he is refused early decision. At this time, he can elect to be put on a regular admissions status and apply to other schools as well.

The advantage of this policy is in releasing the student, if accepted, from the wear and tear of worry and uncertainty. For the college, it guarantees entry of a small but select group of highly desirable students.

The disadvantage to the student is sometimes in limiting the choice of college unnecessarily and before a valid first choice is made. At this writing we have two students who are applying for early decision. One is highly qualified, has made extensive inquiry about other schools, and has no questions as to her first choice. The early decision program was made for her. The other student has been vacillating between choice of school and program for some time and is still undecided as to whether he wants business, liberal arts, or engineering. For him, the early decision program is too limiting. He should apply to several colleges and come to a decision later in the year after further college visits and the passage of time make the ultimate decision easier.

If the student is a scholarship candidate, he should send in the widely-used Parents Confidential Statement of the Educational Testing Service in the fall. The applications are supplied to the high school by request. Reports of his financial need will then be circulated to the colleges he indicates. Some colleges use their own application forms. The student should check the college catalogs as to the correct procedure. In any case, the application for scholarship aid from colleges should be completed in the fall.

COLLEGE PLACEMENT SERVICES

After the acceptances roll in, there are usually always one or two youngsters who were turned down by *all* the schools to which they applied. Sometimes the counselor can anticipate this. Sometimes it comes as a rude shock. Whatever the reason for the necessity of late applications, there is still hope.

There are always vacancies in good colleges at this time for *qualified* applicants. And there are several nonprofit agencies that provide the service of getting the late applicant and college together. The colleges report their vacancies to the admission centers, describing the qualifications of the candidate they want or will take. The student applies to the center, outlining in brief the type of school he wants, completes a questionnaire, and encloses a transcript and a small fee ($15-$25). The center acts as a clearing house—sending the credentials of the student to those schools where the student would seem to belong by reason of interest and ability. If the college feels the student is qualified, it will offer admittance. Thousands of students are successfully placed each year through these services. And the list of cooperative colleges includes many top quality schools. Following are a few of the better known services.

> College Admissions Center, 610 Church St., Evanston, Illinois 60201
>
> College Admission Assistance Center, 41 E. 65th St., New York, New York 10021
>
> Catholic College Admissions & Information Center, 3805 McKinley St., N.W., Washington, D.C.
>
> American College Admissions Advisory Center, Junto School Building, 12th & Walnut Sts., Philadelphia, Pa. 19107

While we have been talking in terms of college admission, the same procedure is followed in the choice of and application to various types of schools. Here again, it is important that the student consult the catalogs and, if possible, visit the school.

Financing an education

It is true that there are increasing opportunities for financial aid to needy students. This is fortunate because college costs are constantly rising. Imagine paying $3,000 a year for your child's education! However, it is well to keep in mind that the more expensive schools are also the ones that usually have the most generous scholarship programs. This is a sort of Robin Hood policy of taking from the rich and giving to the poor. However, less affluent colleges also have scholarship programs of significance. Moreover, there are numerous other sources of financial aid. The following is designed to suggest some possibilities.

COLLEGE SCHOLARSHIP

Loans, campus jobs and financial grants-in-aid are available in most colleges and are the chief source of financial help for students. Aid is given primarily on the basis of need, but since there seldom is enough money to go around, financial aid is competitive. The student who promises to be most successful on the basis of his record will stand the best chance of receiving substantial aid. However, many youngsters who are good scholarship candidates are scared away from many a college by the prospect of high costs and uncertainty as to financial aid. My approach to these students is to encourage them to apply to these schools in the hope of receiving adequate aid and to also apply to a less expensive school within their financial capacity in the eventuality that the aid does not materialize.

The applicant should consult the college catalog to determine the procedure for making application for aid.

FEDERAL STUDENT ASSISTANCE PROGRAMS

National Defense Loans

Public Law 85-864. In recent years, the National Defense Students Loan Program (enacted in 1958) has provided significant aid to colleges and two-year schools. In 1964 a total of 1,547 colleges in all 50 states participated in this program.

Briefly, the program works as follows. The government distributes funds among the participating colleges which contribute an amount equal to at least ⅑ of the federal fund. The college assumes the responsibility of administering the loans, which can be up to $1,000 in any one year (average around $500), $5,000 total. Any full-time student in good standing and in need is eligible. Special consideration is given to teacher candidates and science, math, engineering or language majors. Repayment of the loan begins one year after completion of the full-time course and extends over a ten-year period during which interest of 3 per cent per annum accrues. Repayment and interest charges are waived during periods of service in the armed forces or further full-time education. In the case of those going into teaching, 50 per cent of the loan becomes a gift at the rate of 10 per cent for each year of teaching for five years. The borrower's obligation is cancelled in case of death or total disability.

Although many millions of dollars are involved, the loan fund is still competitive. Not every applicant can receive aid. As with most scholarships, academic promise and performance are important qualifications. Although one doesn't need to be on the Dean's List to qualify, the higher the rank, the better the chances. Perhaps it would be better to say that a barely passing student would stand a poor chance of receiving aid, while his C+ roommate might very well qualify.

Federal Work-Study Programs

Public Law 88-452. This provides a program of part-time campus jobs for needy full-time students. The federal share of funds for compensation is 75 per cent, the balance furnished by the college.

Educational Opportunity Grants

Public Law 89-329. This provides federal funds for students who would otherwise be financially unable to attend the college of their choice. The grants depend on the amount of aid the applicant receives from the college at which he is enrolled and from other sources. The grants will match these contributions up to a maximum of $800 and are renewable for four years. The grant may be increased by $200 if the student ranks in the upper half of his class for the last three years.

In addition, there are federal programs providing funds for graduate work to assist students intending to teach in either college, secondary or ·elementary schools, plus funds for traineeships (seniors only) and graduate fellowships in the training of handicapped children (Educational Assistance Act).

In each of the programs described above, applications should be made to the college through its student financial aid office.

Veteran Benefits

Public Law 89-358. This law provides benefits for veterans of the armed forces who have served on active duty a minimum of

180 days and were discharged after January 31, 1955. Benefits amount to $100 per month for single students; married students receive more according to the number of dependents. Applicants should check with the nearest Veterans Administration office for details.

The War Orphan's Educational Assistance Act provides financial aid to dependents of deceased veterans of World War II or the Korean Conflict. Contact your local VA office for information.

Amvet's Memorial Scholarships provide aid as above.

PRIVATE SCHOLARSHIPS

We have already mentioned the National Merit Scholarships which are supported by contributions from corporations and industries. Many other national scholarships are available but are extremely competitive. For example, the General Motors National Scholarship plan is one of GM's several programs in advancing higher education. The recipients are selected by those colleges participating in the program.

Labor is increasing their financial assistance to needy candidates in higher education. AFL-CIO member unions distribute thousands of dollars each year to students in their areas.

Business and industry is also expanding their aid programs, particularly to sons and daughters of their employees. The Ford Motor Co., several paper industries, the food store chains and aircraft industries are just a few examples. I suggest that the counselor canvass the larger businesses and industries in his area to determine what opportunities exist.

State Scholarships

Almost all states provide some type of financial aid to education, varying from outright grants to guaranteed loan funds administered through banks. Students and counselors are advised to write to their state Department of Education for information. A fact to remember is that the low tuition of state colleges and universities is in itself a scholarship.

Local Scholarships

Most communities provide scholarship aid through industries, fraternal orders, service clubs, women's clubs, etc. The counselor should compile this information together with information on state and federal programs and publish a mimeographed brochure for the use of parents and students.

COOPERATIVE WORK-STUDY PLANS

Many colleges have developed cooperative work-study programs where the student spends alternate semesters studying at the campus and working in a job related to his field. The college provides the job placement service with cooperating businesses and industries. This program lengthens the time necessary to attain the degree by one year, but the student is better able to work his way through college and gains valuable practical experience at the same time. The various college guides furnish a list of colleges and universities which operate a cooperative program. Students should write for full particulars.

TUITION PAYMENT PLANS, BANK LOANS, ETC.

Many banks provide loans that can be repaid in monthly payments. For the family that will have to pay educational expenses out of earned income, this program can be helpful. Of course, as we all know only too well, you pay for the service.

Some states guarantee the amount of a loan to banks, which permits lower interest rates. Students must be in good standing in college to qualify.

I suggest that counselors inquire of their friendly neighborhood banker for information on these and other possibilities.

Since it is impossible to list or even be aware of the larger number of general and special scholarships, I suggest that the counselor keep several reference books on hand. I recommend *How to Beat the High Cost of College* by Claire Coy as the best general discussion. on financing an education in all its aspects that I have seen. For a complete listing I recommend Feingold's *Scholarships, Fellowships and Loans,* Volumes 1, 2 and 3. *Need a Lift?* published annually by the American Legion is another helpful compilation.

ORGANIZING A LOCAL SCHOLARSHIP PROGRAM

Despite the large amount of scholarship aid from every conceivable source, there is still not enough money to go around. Top students have little difficulty in financing the college of their choice, but there remains a large category of average college students who may not qualify for substantial help. These students are worth helping—they will comprise the backbone of the nation. Among them are potential statesmen, business leaders, industrialists, and maybe even one or two college presidents. So the counselor ought to look for any available money for his counselees.

One of the best ideas to come to light recently—and one that is in the best tradition of American community action—is the Citizen's Scholarship Foundation, Inc. Born as the brain child of Dr. Irving Fradkin, a Fall River, Massachusetts, dentist, this national organization has mushroomed with spectacular vigor and success. Each local chapter is organized by volunteer workers to raise money for needy students and to award scholarships that are actually, though not legally, interest-free loans. Bylaws may vary, but usually, to be eligible, a student should be in the top half of his class and be accepted by a school of higher learning. This includes college, two-year schools, nursing schools, etc. One of the important features of this program is that it provides a single coordinating agency to administer all scholarships. It also serves as a convenient coffer for an individual contribution of a dollar (the organization's slogan is "dollars for scholars") or a gift of $1,000. The local chapter is highly organized into committees to manage the solicitation of business, industry, private homes, professional men, special gifts, existing scholarship, etc. A scholarship committee is charged with the selection of candidates according to an impersonal and fair rating scale with need as the prime factor. The national office will supply full descriptive particulars with instructions for incorporating, money-raising, ideas, application forms and all kinds of helpful information. Write to Citizen's Scholarship Foundation of America, Inc., 100 Purchase Street, Fall River, Massachusetts.

If your community needs such an organization, there is no more important nor compelling community activity for a counselor than to initiate the formation of such a project. I suggest you start with an already existing group that is active and community minded. In our town, it was the Junior Chamber of Commerce that picked up the challenge. Most service organizations are eager to espouse a worthy cause. This particular cause is easy to sell because most of the questions are already answered. If your town is too small, enlist the cooperation of neighboring towns. Write to the national office in Fall River for párticulars and do your homework. Then, if you pick the right organization, you will find your ideas readily accepted. Once the program has been adopted and put into operation, my advice to the counselor is to restrict his activities to a minor role. It puts the counselor in an embarrassing position to be too closely identified with the distribution of scholarship funds.

Public or private school?

From time to time the counselor in the public schools will be faced with the question of whether or not one of his counselees should transfer to a college preparatory boarding school. This introduces the whole topic of private vs. public school. Private schools are primarily Eastern institutions, but excellent "prep" schools are located throughout the country. Good private schools offer excellent instruction in the best of learning environments. They offer a variety of activities—intellectual, artistic and athletic. Small classes insure individualized teaching; supervised evening study hours make daily preparation an accepted part of learning by the student. Private school teachers claim—with some reason— that they can exert more of an influence on the youngster by having him 24 hours a day, in contrast to the six- or seven-hour public school day. The atmosphere is one of purpose: educational attainment and, for most, college entrance.

In view of this, why should there be any question—beyond that of expense—whether any boy or girl might not be better off in a private school? Well, first of all, it is an artificial environment where the student is spoon-fed and constantly supervised. It substitutes a faculty for a family, and I'm old-fashioned enough to think that a family is better equipped than a faculty for bringing up a child. Then too, for the lad or lass who has spent four years in a prep school, college becomes merely a boring extension of the same kind of experience. Finally, I think prep school removes the youngster from the realities of life. Everything is too well ordered, well appointed and insular. I would rather have my children rub elbows in his homeroom with the sons and daughters of our less fortunate, culturally deficient, poor families, as well as those of our more affluent "upper class." In this manner, we end up with a bunch of shiny-elbowed kids who not only understand, but are sympathetic with, the problems of the under privileged, regardless of race, color or creed.

So the scales are quite evenly balanced, though I prefer the public school experience for the normal student. I believe the private school can do a superior job with those children who, for a variety of reasons, cannot benefit from high school. These may be the children of parents forced to travel, or from broken homes, or from homes where normal supervision is impossible because of any one of a number of situations. The private school can do a job with the under-achiever, the boy or girl who is too immature to generate the self-discipline necessary to succeed in public school. Some prep schools are concentrating on these youngsters, offering a post-graduate year. This has worked out well for a number of our graduates.

I hope I don't give the impression that private schools are for the problem kids. The vast majority of students in these schools are normal, very intelligent, well-adjusted girls and boys whose families believe in the tradition of a prep school-college background. I happen to be a champion of the public school experience and my advice to parents when asked, is to keep the child in public school if the quality of public education in the community is satisfactory and if the child is developing well scholastically and socially. Studies have shown that the qualified high school graduate, after the initial adjustment to the college pace, does as well or better than his prep school trained classmate. Indeed, the fact that the prep school graduate is so well advanced is sometimes an irresistible invitation to coast too long in college, to take advantage of new-found freedoms, and to sometimes "come a cropper." This experience, of course, is not limited to private school products but it is one of their acknowledged problems.

It has been my observation that boys adjust to the monastic routine of the boarding school better than girls. The activities provided are more suited to the sports-conscious, socially more immature boy. I am oversimplifying again and, like any apprehensive male, taking refuge in generalities. I know of many fine girls' schools full of many happy kids (including my nieces). But, I still stand by my original statement. Boys generally are happier than girls in the boarding school situation.

If a family has decided to transfer their child to a private school, they should be aware of certain facts. First of all, good private schools are highly selective. They, like the colleges, react to the oversupply of applicants by demanding high scholastic performance, excellent personal qualifications and a large bankroll. Most boarding school costs are equivalent to the costs of independent colleges. At the same time, scholarships are often available. Many schools require the Secondary School Tests of the CEEB. In view of all this, an early visit to the school is recommended. With the exception of those schools that specialize in post-graduate years, most private schools discourage the one-year student. I recommend Sargent's *Handbook of Independent Schools* for the counselor's bookcase, along with a number of private school catalogs.

There is another class of private schools: those for exceptional children—the handicapped, emotionally disturbed, etc. These tend to be expensive and, in their own way, selective. As a resource reference I suggest Sargent's *Schools for Exceptional Children* as a valuable source of information to the counselor.

Summary

This chapter has attempted to describe some of the philosophical and practical aspects of school counseling and placement. I have indicated that a wide knowledge of schools and colleges is a necessary tool of the counselor. To acquire this knowledge takes a few years of experience, but school choice is one of the areas in which the counselor's talents and knowledge are most needed. We should leave nothing to chance in making sure that all qualified applicants go on to further education or training. For many, the limiting factor may be financing an education. Accordingly, the counselor should familiarize himself with the variety of national, state, and local programs of financial aid. This is one more example of my concept of the academically oriented guidance program. Let's be concerned, *really* concerned, with education in all its forms.

Bibliography

On college admissions:

How to be Accepted by the College of Your Choice, Dr. Benjamin Fine, Channel Press Inc., Great Neck, N.Y.

A Handbook for Counselors of College Bound Students, Association of College Admission Counselors, Evanston, Illinois.

Manual of Freshman Class Profiles, Educational Testing Service, Princeton, N.J.

Guides to Colleges:

Lovejoy's College Guide, Lovejoy's Vocational School Guide, Simon and Schuster, New York

Barron's Profiles of American Colleges, Benjamin Fine, Barron's Educational Series, Inc., Woodbury, N.Y.

A Comparative Guide to American Colleges, James Case and Max Birnbaum, Harper and Row, N.Y. and Evanston, Ill.

The College Blue Book, Vol. 1., the College Blue Book, Yonkers, N.Y.

Scholarship Information:

How to Beat the High Cost of College, Claire Coy, Bernard Geis Associates, Distributed by Random House, New York, N.Y.

Scholarships, Fellowships and Loans, Volumes I, II, III, S. Norman *Need a Lift?* The American Legion, Dept. S.P.O., Box 1055, Indianapolis, Indiana 46206, Feingold, Bellman Publishing Co., Cambridge, Mass.

Information on private schools:

Directory for Exceptional Children and Handbook of Private Schools, Porter Sargent, 11 Beacon St., Boston, Mass.

Boarding School Directory of the United States, Vol. I., Paul Bauer, Educational Bureau, Inc., Chicago, Ill.

Since most of these books are revised from time to time, ask for the latest edition.

7

Establishing an Effective
Job Placement Program

And into the Cold, Cruel World

There is a widespread and naive belief among laymen that the counselor's job is to sit down with a child, give a series of tests, and somehow come up with a career choice which the child will adopt and follow happily and prosperously ever after. At the same time most parents seem downright apologetic if their son or daughter has no concrete career plan in mind upon entering high school. "Here he is 16 years old and no idea at all what he will do!" The assumption is, of course, that the counselor will know. I wish the problem were that simple. Or do I? Certainly it would take some of the fun and adventure out of life if this kind of predestination were possible. However, I have no fears on this score. Vocational guidance is one of the most difficult of the counselor's tasks. This chapter will discuss the procedures and tools available to the counselor and what he can expect to achieve in an attempt to help point his counselees in a direction that promises the most opportunity for a full life.

Career counseling

There are two elements necessary for a wise occupational choice. One is a knowledge of occupations. The other is a knowledge of self.

When one realizes how little the average high school student knows of the world of work, it is not hard to see why teenagers are doubtful of their ultimate adult role. Those that do have a career in mind are usually quite unrealistic. If fate were to encourage their early plans, we would have a nation of first basemen and airline pilots married to fashion models and airline stewardesses, respectively. The counselor *can* do something about that.

But it is even more difficult for a youngster to develop the mature insight necessary for a self-evaluation, even though it is an avowed goal of most guidance programs. Not that we shouldn't try, but in some cases, one has to wait for the individual to grow up before he can formulate realistic occupational goals—or any goals at all.

The logical approach, under the circumstances, is to postpone the ultimate decision as long as possible. One of the reasons for going to college, beyond the primary goal of being *educated,* is to discover more about life, society and self. A junior or senior in college is much better equipped to make an occupational choice than is the high school senior. Indeed, one of the hoped-for results of a real education is that it will make possible the judgments and decisions necessary for career planning. This is another reason why I favor the liberal arts.

Almost all other types of schools and colleges make a choice mandatory in the senior year of high school and are limiting in varying degrees. The engineering school candidate commits himself to a particular kind of education, one that has rather rigidly circumscribed limits. The business administration candidate makes another kind of choice with its limitations. Similarly, but to an even greater degree, prospective nurses, technicians, computer operators and candidates for any specialized school find their choice of jobs limited by the very training they receive. It follows that the counselor will be involved with those students in career counseling which, under the circumstances, is basic to school choice. He will also, of course, counsel those who will enter the labor market directly upon graduation.

There is one fact that should not be overlooked in considering the individual's job choice. Most people would be happy and successful in a variety of occupations, providing there were certain factors common to each. I don't believe that there is such a thing as a single niche in life for people. The lives of so many people show that they can be equally successful in several vocations. Most of our political leaders have had successful careers in law, business or industry.

Nor is the variegated career limited to national figures. My fishing partner has been a successful commercial airplane pilot, construction supervisor, builder and real estate agent. He has enjoyed them all, although he really likes farming best. This would tend to suggest what I feel should be an important item of job counseling: The concept that change is a normal, expected, hardly to-be-avoided fact of life. I will return to this idea later.

Occupational education

Thus far I have been rather negative about the problem of career choice. However, there are some positive steps we can take. Let's consider the first of the elements of occupational choice—knowledge of occupations. How can we inform our counselees about the variety and nature of jobs?

I would hope that this be a planned, progressive program starting in the elementary grades and continuing through junior high to high school. An introductory unit in the sixth grade which surveys the job field in a general way could be most helpful. I would like to see such a unit include:

1. A broad classification of occupations, such as the five categories employed by the California Occupational Inventory: personal-social, natural, mechanical, business, artistic, and scientific.
2. The concept of different levels of jobs within a category and the qualifications and preparation necessary for each level; i.e., engineering, technician, tradesman.
3. The concept of individual differences—interests and aptitudes—and their part in individual occupational choice.

Such a unit should be very general in nature. No attempt

should be made to encourage an individual job choice at this time, although some sixth grade students will formulate tentative goals.

A SIXTH GRADE UNIT ON OCCUPATIONS

The following is a series of ideas which could serve as a basis for a unit in occupations designed for sixth graders. Portions or all of it can be adapted to the needs of a particular school.

General purposes:

1. To stimulate thinking about an eventual job choice.
2. To inform pupils of the various job fields and the relation of abilities, interests and values of job choice.
3. To acquaint pupils with job opportunities in their area.

A. *Introduction to Occupations*

1. Where people work; percentage of working population employed in various job fields as shown by *Occupational Outlook Handbook;* brief discussion of local job categories as indicated by jobs of student's parents (use a written questionnaire).

2. Changes in the nature of occupations: the increase in skilled and semi-skilled jobs as a result of technology. The increasing importance of education.

3. Brief description of job families as categorized by the *California Interest Inventory.*

4. Suggested pupil activity: local survey of occupations. Break down class into committees to investigate the number of individuals, firms and businesses in major categories. Also, the annual turnover and major job categories within the larger firms and industries. How this is to be handled depends upon the size and complexity of business and industry within the community. Considerable ingenuity and coordination is necessary to avoid duplication within a school system. If some prior field work is done, however, key sources of information can be prepared for the onslaught and can have mimeographed material ready for the little eager beavers. These sources might include the Chamber of Commerce, personnel managers of large firms, the employment bureau, the yellow pages of the telephone book, the high school placement service, the town clerk, the superintendent of the local hospital, etc.

Suggested Job Categories:

Personal-social—teachers and administrators, social workers, psychologists and psychiatrists, nurses, YMCA workers, recreation directors, airline hostesses.

Natural—farmers, horticulturists, landscapers, nursery men, florists, tree experts, turf experts (see local golf course), park managers, biologists.

Mechanical—engineers, technicians, machine and tool designers, machinists and machine operators, tradesmen, mechanics and repairmen, truck drivers, airplane pilots.

Business—managers, accountants, bookkeepers, stenographers, general clerical workers, salesmen, real estate and insurance brokers, bankers and tellers, retail store owners and clerks, advertising men.

Artistic—artists, photographers, interior decorators, musicians, teachers of art, music, dance, etc., actors, authors, fashion designers, window decorators, architects.

Scientific—chemists, physicists, technicians, biologists, geologists, meteorologists, medical technicians, X-ray specialists.

Personal Services—barbers, hairdressers, waitresses, bartenders, cooks, gas station attendants, airline hostesses, policemen, firemen, sanitation personnel, custodians.

For small communities with little industry, this activity might be so restricted as to be meaningless beyond the obvious lesson that opportunity might lie outside the immediate area, a significant fact in itself. For large school systems, on the other hand, the task of organization might well be prohibitive.

However, if the nature of the community lends itself to this kind of project, this age group is capable of surprising effort. Of course, one should not expect an accurate survey, but rather a rough picture that will reflect the presence, or absence, of diversified opportunity. A certain amount of selectivity and much imagination are necessary in planning the survey.

If the program is attempted, the guidance director should be willing not only to sell the idea to the sixth grade teachers but to help set up the program and aid in its coordination (the time element again raises its ugly head).

B. *Interests, Abilities and Values in Job Choice*

1. *Jobs and Aptitudes:* give examples of jobs requiring specific abilities, i.e. engineering—math aptitude, ability to analyze, accuracy, etc. List 12 common jobs and ask pupils to list the ability and personality requirements for each.

2. *Jobs and Interests:* refer again to categories in California Occupational Interest Inventory. List six major interest categories and ask pupils to list several jobs under each. Emphasize the difference between interest and ability as well as their changing pattern of interests.

3. *Jobs and Values:* What does the pupil want of life and his job? Discussion of job satisfaction vs. pay.

4. Point out the personal satisfaction in any job well done—at any level. Ask the pupils to write a paper on what they want from their job. What kind of satisfaction? What rewards?

C. *The Levels of Occupations Within a Job Field and the Training Involved*

1. Illustrate the job levels within a category.

> Mechanical: Machine Operator
> Machinist
> Machine Designer
> Engineer

2. Point out the training necessary for each at both secondary school and college levels. Ask the pupils to illustrate similar levels with the other categories of occupations (using the California Occupational Interest Inventory), together with the required training.

D. *Field Trips to Industry and Business Firms*

1. Select a cooperating firm that houses a variety of jobs. Break down the class prior to the visit into small groups that will visit a section of the firm—administration, bookkeeping, sales and advertising, production, engineering, etc. Return to class to pool information. Pupils should be provided with a simple questionnaire to be filled out during the trip, including such items as nature of job observed, training necessary, pay and other rewards. Contrast routine jobs with jobs with varied tasks involving skill and thought. Develop the concept that with responsibility goes higher rewards. It is necessary that the cooperating firm *be informed in advance* as to what information the group is seeking.

2. If a field trip is impossible, set up a sample factory on a chart showing the organization of responsibility.

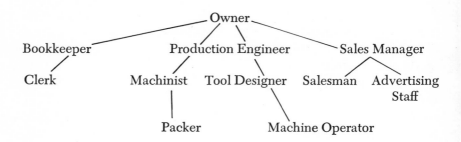

The teacher can provide the type of information asked for by the same questionnaire used in field trips. The pupils should be given an opportunity to give their ideas first, however. Point out the relationship of training, responsibility and pay among the levels of occupations.

3. The organization of the school system can be also used as an example of a type of industry. Point out the similar structure with the superintendent acting as the president, the school board as directors and part owners. The children, of course, are the product, the teachers the production workers, the principals act as production engineers, while custodians, clerks, the school nurse, and lunch room workers, etc., serve as specialists in various occupational fields. The guidance counselors—the most unproductive of all—correspond to personnel managers.

This little hierarchy can easily be used to illustrate the variety of jobs and responsibilities found in any business or industry. And the thought that "teacher" is on the lowest level of the hierarchy should be gratifying to the pupils. I jest, of course.

CAREER PLANNING IN THE SECONDARY SCHOOL

Junior high or freshman year of high school is the time for a second planned assault. If the school has a group guidance class, the study of occupations should be a major unit leading to choice of high school program.

Ideally, the fall of the eighth grade is my choice of the best time to schedule such a unit. In a later chapter, we'll discuss the group guidance classes in detail. For now, it will suffice to say that the contemplated unit should be quite general at the beginning, but become more personal as it progresses until a *tentative* goal may be reached by many. Again I remind the reader that, even after these attempts to inform, the majority of the students, still children, are incapable of mature judgment and all job choices should be considered as temporary—both by the student and the counselor. The approach of the student should be to make a tentative job choice if he so desires, then keep an open mind. The youngster should feel no pressure on him to make a choice. The purpose of the unit is to inform, not to limit. The unit should emphasize the fact that education and training widens the variety of job opportunities available to a student and makes it possible for him to work at a higher level within a job field.

If a school system has no group guidance classes, this unit could be scheduled in social studies classes. In many ways, this approach may be better. Guidance classes, since they ordinarily receive no credit towards graduation, lack authority and sometimes, I'm afraid, lack importance in the minds of youngsters conditioned to the reward system of marks.

I have previously mentioned a "Career Corner" located in the school library where school catalogs and college guides are available to pupils. To complete this, an adequate supply of occupational information material should also be provided. I suggest several copies of the *Occupational Outlook Digest* as the basis for such a collection. Timely articles from periodicals, magazines and newspapers can be included. This is a good place for a display rack which can house the mass of occupational material that passes over the counselor's desk.

Beyond this point, I believe that the significant work in job choice will be accomplished by individual guidance conferences initiated in the junior year and culminating in the choice of schools or jobs in the senior year.

To summarize, the process of teaching occupational information should start with generalizations intended to inform, should encourage the pupil to think about jobs and himself, and should postpone as long as possible the ultimate decision. The obvious reason for this approach is to allow the student to experience life as long as possible so that his final choice will be based on mature self-analysis.

Self-evaluation

This brings us to the second element in job choice: self-appraisal. How can we assist the student in arriving at a mature evaluation of his potential and his limitations?

Of course, the youngster has been measured and graded during all his school years and, by the time he enters high school, he has a fair idea of his scholastic ability in comparison to his classmates. He also is aware that he has developed some interests and skills. But as for the more subtle personality evaluations, most students are quite unaware of what they are as developing individuals, or *how they compare with others*. This is complicated by the fact that they are not now what they will be in four years. It is very difficult for them to anticipate the changes maturity will bring in their attitudes, degree of self-confidence or in their increasing ability to cope with situations. This, probably, is the chief stumbling block in occupational counseling. The danger is always in encouraging a choice that is based solely on the student's present state of development. *Occupational decisions should not be limiting.* I remind the reader of the philosophy expressed in an earlier chapter—we schedule according to ability, not according to occupational interest, and in such a way as to leave all doors open. The same approach applies to job choice. In fact, the two ideas are actually two facets of the same problem—the changing, developing individual.

It is possible to stimulate high school students to start a process of introspection. Certainly, they are sufficiently absorbed in themselves to react readily to an invitation to examine themselves further. In the occupational unit described above for the secondary school, some time should be spent in pointing out the personality requirements of various occupations: The engineer versus the research scientist, the salesman as compared with the accountant, the teacher and the librarian. Always, in such discussions, the student should be reminded that he is developing, that he will soon be capable of more than he is now. Most youngsters are so unsure, so afraid of their ability to assume the adult role! They need constant encouragement and assurance from parents, teachers and counselors.

Individual conferences provide opportunities to encourage students to indulge in introspection. For example, Mary wants to go into nursing, but she is failing biology. Why is she failing? Is it because it lacks interest for her? Is it because she is unwilling to do the considerable drill work necessary to memorize? Is she unduly squeamish at the idea of dissection, at the sight of blood or untidy viscera? These questions can stimulate some worthwhile self-appraisal—if Mary is mature enough to face up to reality. Sometimes Mary is still too much of a child to be willing to undergo such a self-analysis. However, to start such an appraisal —a recognition of facts—is half the battle, regardless of whether Mary can do something positive about the problem at the moment. If she *can* react positively, she is really growing up and she is the counselor's delight!

The personality scale of the *Kuder Preference Test* can be used to stimulate an awareness of the personal qualifications of jobs, but only in a general way. Again, I warn the reader of the danger of an evaluation based on this stage of incomplete development that is characteristic of the average high school youngster.

There are tests of general aptitudes but, like the interest inventory, I believe they are more useful for the mature individual. Furthermore, they test aptitudes and skills that, for all their importance at lower levels of job fields, don't seem to apply to higher levels. In any case, they do not measure the intangibles that make for success or satisfaction in any job. Because of these limitations and because they are expensive and difficult to administer, I feel that they have little value in the average high school.

We should not lose sight of the fact that much of what these aptitude tests show is already suggested by the information on the youngster's permanent record. We should have a fair idea of a student's general intelligence, his verbal and mathematical ability. His subject grades in bookkeeping, stenography, etc. will indicate clerical ability. To a degree, space relations can be measured by success in geometry and mechanical drawing. Finger and manual dexterity may be demonstrated in stenography, band, clothing, shop, typing, art, etc. I wonder if we might not get as accurate a picture of aptitudes from a careful study of the pupil's school performance as from the artificial situation of the test. In any case, I have not found aptitude tests particularly helpful.

There is one exception to the above. We have the G.A.T.B. (General Aptitude Test Battery—see Chapter 4) administered to certain seniors by the local division of the Employment Security Office. These are seniors who are planning to go directly into the job market and who show no particular abilities or interests. For these, their patterns of response may suggest realistic job choices as well as stimulate interest in these same jobs. The division also assists in job placement of these individuals as part of the total program.

PROGRAMS AND PRACTICES

Career days can be useful, but they too have their limitations and can easily be overdone. The problem here is double-barreled. To make such a program interesting and effective, students should have some idea of their occupational interests. Yet many students in high school still are in the dark on this score. So the program also becomes a means of informing these students as to career opportunities. How to present a variety of occupations to a group is a problem. Any one occupation will attract the attention of a segment of the audience. The others will understandably be bored stiff. *This is the underlying problem with all attempts at presenting occupational information.* It is a kind of vicious circle.

In our school, we have worked with the Chamber of Commerce in presenting a different kind of "Career Day" every other year. Students are first given a checklist to fill out in homeroom indicating broad fields of occupational interest. We then set up a series of five assemblies, each of which features a panel of four or five speakers who discuss selected occupations. We try to get good speakers who can interest the whole school to a degree. This, of course, is the key to success. After this series of assemblies, we set up a "Career Day" (actually a lengthened homeroom period) when the students have a chance to visit in small groups with the representative of that occupation in which they have indicated an interest. The details of scheduling and control are difficult to set up and very time consuming. But the total value of the program probably warrants the effort. The problem of occupational choice is dramatized, the community is brought closer to the school, and it furthers good public relations. Furthermore, some pupils (it's hard to evaluate this) are bound to profit from the experience and move closer to an identification of their own occupational goals. We would be the first to admit that this is not the whole answer to the problem. Indeed, I doubt if the complete answer exists at all.

Field trips to industry and business can also be useful, but one runs up against much the same problems here. Who goes where and on what basis is the decision made? Probably the most successful of such programs that I have seen is one created by our industrial arts (shop) teacher who requires a visit to an industry as a requirement of his courses. These are small group or individual visits which he arranges with cooperating industries. There is a definite goal in mind for each student at the beginning, and the student is required to write a report including the answers to questions that apply to his particular case. Such a program is highly personal, well organized and has the best chance of success.

Our business course students participate in a N.O.M.A (National Office Managers Association) program each year by which they visit the offices of a nearby insurance company to learn more about office jobs and opportunities.

It would seem that such field trips are most effective if the group attending has a broad occupational interest in common and if prior goals are formulated. It also helps if the experience is part of the course requirement—not just an invitation to a lark. A small school can make good use of these programs. A large school may well find the mechanics of organization and the general disruption of the school routine such as to discourage the idea.

One thing that we can all do is to develop a "stable" of resource people in the community who are willing to discuss the occupations they represent with students. Every community has its complement of professional men, accountants, machine designers, chemists, nurses and businessmen. Most are quite happy to give some time to students. We should do more of this.

Experience with an occupation—actual participation in a job—

is the best source of occupational information for anyone. For nursing candidates, the "Green Girl" program is excellent. These girls work as assistants in a variety of ways in the hospital, carrying trays, performing simple patient care and providing all manner of nonprofessional services. It gives them a good look at the nursing profession and some of the less glamorous aspects of nursing.

At our school, we instituted a teacher's aide program where prospective teaching candidates were able to visit nearby elementary schools during study hall time. They acted as observers and assistants to cooperating teachers. This was most successful, but it meant that a student needed to be scheduled for two study periods in a row in order to have the time necessary to make it worthwhile. With our presently crowded school, scheduling difficulties forced us to abandon the program. We will return to it as soon as possible.

We have not yet developed our placement service to the point where we can place a youngster in a part-time job in his chosen occupational field. I suppose this is too much to expect to be able to do in most communities, but it would be a valuable opportunity for job experience if it were possible. I believe that more cooperation with the community could expand the possibilities of all such programs involving actual experience in the field.

CAREER COUNSELING WITH INDIVIDUALS

The programs and procedures outlined above are designed to give the youngster a background for a personal choice. Usually a final commitment is made as a result of a series of visits with the counselor in the junior and senior years of high school.

In the spring of their junior year, we routinely schedule conferences with students to initiate specific plans for post-high school experience. At that time the question, "What are you going to do after high school?" is raised. For many it will obviously be more school. In this case, occupational choice may determine school choice. The choice between engineering, business administration and liberal arts colleges involves the question of ultimate career—except that, for the liberal arts candidate, the choice can be happily postponed. Discussion as to the appropriateness of the other types of higher education raises the question of what is an engineer, an accountant, a business executive, etc. What is the nature of the job? What kind of personal and aptitude qualifications are desirable? This is the point to refer the student to the source materials available in the occupational library. At this time the student might benefit with a talk with a resource person in the field. If the original choice is reinforced by this additional information, we start talking about choice of specific colleges. The same procedure would be followed in the case of a preliminary choice of any school.

Many students, as late as their senior year, are unsure of their job interests and of their ability to qualify. For these students, the counselor will have to initiate an individual program of self-evaluation and education in occupations. Obviously, there has to be a starting point and, if the counselor knows the student, there are bound to be some clues.

For those with the capacity to benefit from the liberal arts, it becomes a matter of interesting the youngster in the prospect of college and of showing him the advantages and possibilities of an education. This may involve a discussion of financing or it may be a matter of bolstering the student's self-confidence.

For anything else, an immediate career choice is necessary. For those in the business course, the natural suggestion is to go on to further education in the field, but at the higher level that such advanced training will make possible. If the business student is unwilling or unable to go on to school, then a discussion of specific jobs is in order. The counselor should know what categories of jobs are ordinarily available in his area and be able to talk in specifics. The student then becomes a job candidate and will come under the placement program in the senior year. For this student, visits to offices and businesses ordinarily hiring from the high school are helpful. Ability and the school academic record are often limiting factors and the student should be reminded that he is already in competition for a job, even while he is attending high school.

The student who likes shop and mechanical drawing can be introduced to the idea of machine design, electronics, architectural design, and similar careers taught in technical schools. If the student doesn't have the courses and ability in math to qualify at that level, he can consider the trades and the prospect of a trade school post-graduate course.

The girl who likes clothing or foods can explore the possibilities in various forms of home economics and the schools appropriate to her academic ability.

The talented artist and musician have undoubtedly already formulated plans for continuing in this field, but there remains the question of what they want to do with their talent: teach? perform? and at what level? There is much to discuss both as to careers and schools.

However, there still remains a number of students who have no inkling of their direction. For these, a good starting point is the profile of the *Occupational Interest Inventory* (taken in the eighth or ninth grade). It serves as a means of stimulating introspection. Is the student still interested in mechanical things? Does he still want to work with his hands or with people? Or have his interests changed? What does this suggest? How has he changed? What training opportunities are available to him? The counselor can suggest possible careers. The student can then consult the occupational library. If at all possible, the parents should be brought into the picture at some point. The responsibility for occupational and school choice rests with the student and the family. It is possible for the counselor to do too much. His role is to suggest possibilities, to secure information, and to avoid forcing his ideas on the pupil. These decisions are highly personal. We would be usurping an authority and pretending an omniscience that we don't possess if we were to play a role more directive than common sense would dictate.

There is one final idea that should be explored at this point. I have mentioned that change is an expected, normal fact of life. It is extremely important to convince students of this. Part of this concept is the idea that failure is also a normal, expected phase of anyone's experience. Kids are so afraid of failure! If we can get them to accept the idea that to try and fail is not disgraceful but merely normal, we would be providing a really significant service. To try and to fail is in many cases noble. To be afraid to try, to avoid a challenge—this shrinks the spirit and fosters discontent.

I refer to my approach of school placement—aim high. Encourage these high school kids to stretch themselves, to expand their opportunities. Don't let them vegetate in a dull, boring rut of mediocrity—and I mean mediocrity as measured by their potential.

But to aim high is to be ready and willing to accept the consequences of failure. This is hard for most people to accept—I include myself. We can help as counselors, teachers and parents by fostering the idea of accepting a challenge and by avoiding recrimination and guilt feelings if the youngster fails to meet the challenge. It should be "Good try! At least you had the guts to attempt something different and you grew a little bit in the process." This last is a prayerful suggestion to parents for whom I have a heartfelt sympathy.

Sources of occupational information

Any well-appointed guidance suite will house a complete and up-to-date library of occupational information. There are numerous services which provide such libraries. The Science Research Associates and Chronicle Guidance Service, for example, are well-known occupational information services. These organizations will supply a complete library plus a periodical mailing to update the material. But before the counselor invests a sizable slice of the community's money in such a set—and they are expensive—consider the *Occupational Outlook Handbook*, published periodically by the United States Department of Labor. This paperback volume includes descriptions, qualifications, training, employment outlook, working conditions and pay of nearly 700 occupations. It is well organized, indexed and extremely easy to use. In recent years, we have used this single book almost to the exclusion of the more impressive file of occupational monographs and pamphlets. Maybe it shouldn't supplant the more extensive and detailed information found in the occupations library, but it certainly is useful, handy and there is no need to rummage through a file.

Many guidance offices use the *Dictionary of Occupational Titles* published by the U.S. Department of Labor in four volumes. It is quite detailed and the most complete of all the volumes and libraries mentioned. It includes over 25,000 job descriptions together with the training and qualifications of each occupation or group of closely related occupations.

There are numerous other sources of occupational information. The bibliography of any standard text will suggest these sources. In my opinion, the material suggested above would be more than adequate for most high school guidance programs. The problem is not how to secure the material but how to get it to the student.

Value formation

Underlying the problem of occupation choice and the youngster's concept of his adult role is the formation of worthwhile values. What does the child want out of life? This is a difficult question for a teenager to answer. Can most of us?

In a society which, on the surface at least, becomes more and more materialistic, it is no wonder that a certain segment of our young society has rejected the Cadillac as a symbol of success. The young rebels, the hippies, the draft card burners are all symptoms of a dissatisfaction with society's ethics and values, a dissatisfaction shared by many of their elders. Alcohol, L.S.D. and "pot" are disturbing elements in the rebellion, as are the passivity, lack of purpose and hedonism that are the hallmarks of the more extreme rebels. But, as parents and educators, we must do more than condemn; after all, we have given them little reason not to rebel.

On the other hand (and it is perhaps a more serious problem), the majority of youngsters seem to accept the values of materialism. We live in an affluent society which will not allow a person to starve, to go without medical aid, which protects, assists, and mothers its people as no society in history has done before. Not that we don't have the poor, the suffering, the deprived. But for the average high school kid, the "Golden Age" is here. "Why work? Why knock yourself out? Now is the time for man to enjoy the fruits of his technological genius. Let's enjoy it, gang." Too many high school kids have the time, money and freedom to do just that. The danger is that for them this can become the goal in life—to get a job which will provide them with the means to continue to live the "good life" to which they have become accustomed.

What can we do? My suggestion to the parent is that he become somewhat less permissive and insist that his child earn his privileges. But this is not enough. We must all sell the young people on the idea that there is something more to life than bikinis and wine skins (not that there is anything wrong with them, either). Of course, the first step is to believe this ourselves. The second step is to open up communications with our teenagers. We should all listen more. We should avoid making judgments, but we should not shun voicing our reasons for believing as we do. We should try to understand why teenagers feel as *they* do and accept them for what they are. We don't have to accept their ideas, but we should be ready *to provide valid reasons and facts to support our own.*

As counselors, we should be ready to listen without implying a judgment. We cannot *impose* our values on our counselees. We should be able to supply facts—not emotions—to such problems as L.S.D. and premarital sexual relations. As suggested above, we have a responsibility to see that a child is exposed to experiences, such as the liberal arts, that will promote thought and introspection. In our discussions of schools and occupations, we should dwell on the individual's personal goals. What, indeed, does he want out of life? To make money and live comfortably? To play a role in helping society improve? To lead, to follow, or merely to watch from the sidelines? How to *fulfill* himself?

This idea of self-fulfillment is the ultimate guidance goal of many modern writers on guidance, although it may be expressed in different ways. It is a laudable goal. But it is not a goal restricted to guidance. It is the goal of society and all of its agencies: the family, the school and the church. For this reason, and because I feel that no guidance program can accomplish this goal by itself, I have restricted myself in this book to the more readily attainable goals—sometimes termed intermediate goals—of a service-giving nature. And I feel strongly that these are justifiable goals for the counselor.

However, we should contribute where we can, directly and indirectly, to the formation of worthwhile values and the self-discovery and self-fulfillment of all our students. This should be a concern, even though not a goal, of every counselor and of the entire educational process.

The placement program

Most high schools have developed part-time and full-time placement services as a natural result of their concern with occupational choice. Furthermore, employers are constantly calling the school in search of employees. The busy principal naturally refers them to the guidance counselors who should be the ones best fitted to make the recommendation. Thus a placement service is born.

Although all counselors will be involved in placement, I recommend that one counselor be assigned the responsibility of coordinating the program (see Chapter 9). This avoids duplication of work and promotes an efficient operation.

Part of this counselor's job should be to familiarize himself with the job opportunities in the area. This may entail a survey of local business and industry. We did this some years ago. The counselors divided up the major concerns and visited most in person. A simple questionnaire was completed with the aid of a company official which gave us a good picture of the nature of the jobs performed, training and qualifications of special jobs, pay and rate of turnover. The questionnaires were mailed to those firms we could not visit. We received excellent cooperation. The project was time consuming but informative. We pooled our information and each of us was able to formulate a fairly comprehensive picture of the city's job potential. The local Chamber of Commerce was most helpful and cooperative in supplying lists and names of personnel to contact.

In recent years, we have attempted to expand our contacts with potential employers. I believe the placement counselor should spend some time each year visiting businesses and industries— to inform prospective employers of the kind of product the school trains, as well as to determine what kinds of people the employer wants to hire.

I suggest keeping a file on students who are looking for jobs. Such a file should contain the usual personal information. I also suggest that rank in class and grades in key subjects be included along with a summary of the attendance record. We use a "job request" form that constitutes an "active" file. This shows the nature of the job, name, address and telephone number of the firm, whom to contact, and what students were recommended to apply. When the position is filled, the pertinent information is transferred to a more permanent file. For those of you who can't take the time to maintain an elaborate file, these job request forms can act as the permanent file.

One of the biggest headaches in placement is the inevitable situation when the youngster you recommended quits on short notice—or doesn't show up for work some day. Somehow, we have to sell these kids on the idea of personal responsibility and their obligation to both the employer and the school. I suppose the most we can do is to emphasize this to our counselees. I know our business department hammers away on this subject of ethics, but as with all such pearls of wisdom, they sometimes fall on deaf ears (to confuse a metaphor). We have to take the responsibility for our recommendations, so an honest appraisal is an insurance for both the employer and the reputation of the placement service.

We recently borrowed an effective placement device from a neighboring school. In June, we publish, through the Chamber of Commerce, a list of students still looking for jobs. We include grades in significant courses and the nature of the work desired, along with the age of the student. We omit the name; the employer sees only a number. This provides the students with a measure of privacy. The employer calls the guidance office or, if during the summer, the school office, and the student is then referred to the employer. We place many of our students through this means. May I point out that this continuing close cooperation by the Chamber of Commerce is most valuable and is a relationship that we treasure.

I urge the counselor to nurture such contacts with community agencies. The employment bureaus are good people to have on our side, for instance. They usually have considerable information they are glad to share and, in turn, appreciate any information and business we can give them. After all, we are not in competition with them. I know that to build up an effective placement service, it is necessary to take aggressive action. We cannot sit idly by until the phone rings.

THE ARMED FORCES

It used to be a common situation for the counselor confronted with the problem of career planning for an immature or purposeless student to suggest the service as a convenient place in which to grow up—especially since the youngster was faced by the prospect of military service, anyway.

Experience has borne out the wisdom of such counsel. We have seen so many immature, aimless youths emerge as purposeful, confident young men. The service provides a kind of psychological security where decisions are made for the youngster. He has time to look around and realize that he is as good a man, if not better, than his bunkmates. He soon finds that initiative and industry do pay off. It is a common occurrence to receive reports on our monumental goof-offs who are going to service schools, studying four hours a night, and leading their class.

However, times have changed and, at this writing at least, the service is no longer a very comfortable place. Under the conditions of a shooting war, I hesitate to take the initiative in recommending the service. This is a personal decision for the student. Nevertheless, the counselor has a responsibility to see that his counselees are informed about their military obligations and the ways by which this obligation can be met. For years in our school, we have had a series of assemblies to which representatives of the various branches of the armed forces were invited as guest speakers. We will continue this practice. I feel that how a youngster wishes to handle this problem is a personal decision that depends on many factors. But the counselor can, at least, promote the idea of *planning* for military service. The counselor should be familiar with the obligation the student faces and the various programs currently offered by the various services. Universal military training has been a confusing, somewhat hit or miss proposition and will probably continue to be so whatever changes are made. But in any circumstance, planning is better than drifting.

Some Radical Conclusions

Experience has shown that occupational counseling is a difficult task. The high school student is neither sufficiently informed about the nature of occupations nor capable of projecting himself into the adult world of work. We can provide a certain amount of general information by means of occupational units at different levels and through individual counseling. Occupational choice and school opportunities should be closely connected in such conferences. Talks with representatives of occupations in the community, visits to industries and businesses, and career days can contribute to the student's background of information. Student self-appraisal can sometimes be stimulated, but often time is necessary for the maturation process. Accordingly, career choices should be postponed as long as possible. Job choice should not be limiting, but considered as one opportunity among many available to the youngster.

Basic to occupational choice is value formation. What the individual wants of life should play an important part in his career decision. The counselor should point this out, and the entire school system should concern itself with the formation of worthwhile values. We should avoid *forcing* our own adult values on our teenagers but should be prepared to supply information and facts that contribute to worthy and realistic goals. A school that will listen to the questions and criticism of the young, that will demand high standards of integrity, that places a value on excellence, that respects the student as an individual, and whose faculty serves as an example of an enlightened, cultured adult society can do much to promote the ideals of society.

We seem to be faced with a revolution of culture in our country and in other affluent societies. Easy living has replaced the "Puritan Ethic" of our forefathers, and the last vestiges of Old World culture are fast disappearing. At present, we have not substituted a culture of our own. We seem to be faced instead with a mild state of anarchy. We have, indeed, allowed our children to be disillusioned. Until a truly American culture can emerge—as it eventually will—it is up to us who work with youth to hold the line. I urge a return to an idealistic philosophy. If we believe in such things as basic values—in intrinsically *good* things or *bad* things—we can make our influence felt. I believe in the basic potential in man for nobility. I also believe in the basic weakness of man to revert to his natural animal instincts. Understanding but not permissiveness should be our approach in communicating with young people. Consistency in our own lives and our own values will hopefully be reflected in an acceptance of our system.

Forgive this sermon on the anthill, but the temptation is strong and one goes all to pieces when writing a book. There is always the forlorn hope that somebody will read it and agree.

Bibliography

1. *Occupational Information:*

   *Dictionary of Occupational Titles—*Volumes, Bureau of Employment Security, U.S. Dept. of Labor, Washington, D.C.
   *Occupational Outlook Handbook—*Bureau of Labor Statistics, U.S. Dept. of Labor, Washington, D.C.

   To secure either of the above, write to the Superintendent of Documents, U.S. Government Printing Office, Washington, D.C. 20402

   It may be possible to secure a bibliography of occupational reference material published by the U.S. Dept. of Labor at your local Bureau of Employment Security Office. If not, write to the U.S. Dept. of Labor in Washington, D.C. Local employment offices also have other free materials on occupations.

   Science Research Associates, Inc., Chicago, Illinois.
   Chronicle Guidance, Inc., Moravia, N.Y.

2. *Armed Forces Information:*

   Basic facts about military service. High School news service. Department of Defense, Great Lakes, Illinois.

   Local recruiting offices can also supply the following material:

   U.S. Army Opportunities
   Military Guidance in Secondary Schools
   Navy Occupational Handbook
   Regular NROTC Bulletin
   Navy Waves (Enlisted Women)
   U.S. Air Force Occupational Handbook (For Counselors)
   U.S. Marine Programs—Regular, Reserve, Officer
   U.S. Coast Guard—A Career Service
   For You . . . An Officer's Career in the U.S. Armed Forces
   A New World of Opportunity

8

Techniques in
Group Guidance

Head Shrinking Time

This facetious subtitle was suggested to me by the reaction of a youthful cynic who had just attended a group guidance class in another school in which a group therapy approach to personal problems was being attempted. My concept of group guidance for the average counselor is strictly traditional. I look upon group activity as part of the "planned program" and, primarily, as a method of dispensing information, not as an opportunity for group therapy.

Certainly there is a need for more psychological services in school, and there may be a need for therapeutic counseling in groups. But to me, this seems to be another field, another job, and should not be included among the counselor's responsibilities. We'll come back to this later in the chapter.

In the final analysis, the counselor should try what he thinks he can do—but be ready to evaluate the results impersonally and fairly.

Many group guidance classes have been started and discontinued. Part of the reason for this is administrative. As our schools become more crowded, it is difficult to find the time and space for these programs. Another reason for their disappearance is that it is difficult to conduct an effective group guidance program. But I believe it can be done—and done well.

A group guidance class provides excellent opportunities to impart information to large numbers of individuals at one time. It *should* be a *time-saver*. If it is not, it probably should be discontinued.

There are two points in a student's educational career when he urgently needs information: at the start of high school when he is faced with many choices and again in the senior year when school and career decisions are to be made.

While I've never tried it, I feel that a group guidance approach for seniors and juniors would be advantageous if we could schedule it. I would like to have the juniors during the last half of the year to initiate planning, and the seniors for the first half to implement placement. To do this right, however, would necessitate scheduling according to broad educational and vocational objectives in order to insure a homogeneity of interests. This would be difficult for most schools to accomplish.

Most guidance classes have been developed for eighth or ninth graders where the purposes of the course are more general and deal with educational and vocational information leading up to course planning.

The advantages of group guidance are many. It is possible to present ideas and facts to many students at one time. It offers an opportunity to plan a continuous and developing program with definite aims. Individual conferences are apt to have less continuity and often omit important information. Guidance classes emphasize the importance of planning, provide for group discussion and stimulate questions. They provide a convenient and scheduled place where the counselor can confer with individuals at certain stages on routine matters without disturbing school routine.

There are limitations as well to the group approach. I have emphasized the time element. If the classes demand more than a fifth of the counselor's total school time, I would seriously consider discontinuing them. They should not impair the individual counseling program. I would limit the length of the course to a half year or less, depending on the marking periods of the school. If we limit the course to eighth or ninth graders I would schedule it for the first half for reasons that will become apparent. The classes must be well planned and prepared. Each session should have a definite purpose. Finally, it takes good teaching to make the classes interesting as well as informative. (The audience is immature and has a short attention span.) Anything less is a waste of time. Guidance classes should be run like any subject class, with adequate control, however informal the approach may be.

I have suggested that the unit on occupations might well be included in a social studies course. Such a course does carry more authority in the minds of adolescents and, in many instances, might be more effective than the less formal guidance class. Of course, the teacher has to be sold on the idea. Whether the guidance class or social studies approach is used depends upon the particular school situation.

A group guidance program

The following is a suggested program for ninth grade guidance classes. The general plan is to introduce an occupational unit which is at first general and later more personal, serving as a basis for course planning. It is based on a schedule in which each ninth grader meets once a week for a half-year. The general plan can be slightly revised for eighth graders if desirable.

Week 1. Orientation. Discussion of high school routine, extra-curricular activities, marking system, graduation requirements, etc.

Week 2. Study techniques. I believe that if this material is properly presented, it can be effective. There is certainly a need for it. Most students—even college preparatory seniors—do not know how to study, to organize and memorize. This is important enough to warrant the expenditure of some time. Most books on how to study are too involved and detailed. May I suggest the following for a trial, at least?

I advocate a "write down and test yourself technique." This is nothing new, but the key is in simplifying the procedure and emphasizing time-saving devices.

First, a few chapters of their current social studies text is reproduced on an overhead projector transparency. I project this on one screen and explain the concept of "scanning" to determine the nature of the material and the obvious questions the student will ask himself as he reads the paragraph headings. "What is the Unholy Alliance? Who was Charlemagne? Why did Hannibal cross the Alps? What was he doing with all those elephants?" Next, on a separate transparency with another adjoining projector I show them how I have written down the important ideas under each paragraph heading. I demonstrate how to abbreviate, use words or short phrases which suggest the ideas. We then continue to further paragraphs and I let the students suggest how to list the ideas in each. At the conclusion, I cover up the paragraph notes of each section showing only the paragraph heading and ask them to recall the ideas. I then explain that this is the method they should employ with their own textbook. I make a point that they should keep the worksheets for review purposes and urge them to review daily—not just before a test. (Most won't do this, but some will.) The technique is to learn important ideas first and to include details later.

At the second session, I give them a few minutes to review with their worksheets and then give them a brief quiz on the material we covered. This usually is a convincing demonstration that the method really works. Incidentally, I'm careful not to make the quiz too difficult or I might sabotage the whole project at the outset.

It's possible to carry the idea further and show them how to learn a French vocabulary or the parts of an amoeba. The use of the opaque projectors is an interest-stimulating device and works quite well in keeping their attention. I invite questions and criticism and end up by emphasizing these points.

1. Write down important ideas in "shorthand."
2. Test—make mental notes of omissions or errors.
3. Retest until the material is mastered.
4. Retest as a method of review.
5. Big ideas first—then add details.

I don't dwell on such obvious things as home study conditions, nor do I attempt to discuss notetaking, writing themes, etc. You can easily overdo it.

I know this system works if you can get the youngsters to try it. I realize there are many more points that could be brought into the demonstration, but I purposely keep it brief.

Week 3. Second session of study techniques—quiz and discussion. How to determine important ideas? (Italicized words, questions at end of chapter, teacher emphasis.)

Week 4. Introduction to Occupations. The idea of tentative choices coupled with the assurance of changing interests and increasing potential as students mature. Emphasize the point that the purpose of the unit is to inform; to provide a background of material that they can refer to in the future. Explanation of the necessity for "open-end" course planning and its relation to career planning. Explanation of job fields according to interests, personal-social, natural, mechanical business, artistic and scientific.

Week 6. Break down of job fields into levels, indicating training necessary for each, i.e., *natural field.*

Examples: Farming—2-yr. agricultural school recommended
Forestry—4-yr. course
Wildlife Management—4-yr. college minimum
Entomologist—4-yr. college plus doctorate
Turf Management—2-yr. agricultural school
Marine Biologist—4-yr. college plus doctorate

Week 7. Administration of an interest inventory.

Week 8. Scoring and interpretation of inventory. Point out limitations of the test. Discussion of how the student can use the test in formulating *tentative* goals. Interest vs. ability. Discussion of the possibility of success in more than one job field. Discussion of the possible significance of two high scores, i.e., Mechanical + Scientific = Engineering, Technician, Dentist, etc. Point out necessity of accumulating more information and experience before the student can make a realistic final job choice.

Week 10. Discussion of jobs and their personality requirements, i.e., teaching and librarian, scientist and engineer, machinist and tool designer, doctor and medical technician, etc.

Week 11. Invitation to self-analysis. At this point I asked students to rate themselves on a personality rating test such as the Kuder Personal Reference record or the California Personality Inventory. The purpose of this is to show the relation of personality traits to job choice. The students should be warned in advance that it should not be used to *limit* choice and that they will develop and change in varying degrees. It should emphasize again that any job choices arrived at this point should be tentative.

Weeks 11, 12, 13. Individual job survey. The student surveys an occupation. If the occupational library is extensive enough this can be done in class by individuals or groups according to job interest. If it can't be done in class, I would advise not doing it at all. The purpose here is more to inform pupils about the various features to be considered in a job choice rather than to investigate the occupation itself. The following outline explained in detail in advance can be employed.

Nature of Job—Tasks performed, environment, working conditions, hours, pay, etc.

Training Necessary—School, college, etc. Have students procure names and addresses of two schools that provide the necessary training.

Personal Qualifications—Temperament, talents, skills, physical requirements, mental requirements.

Pay—Both in terms of money and satisfaction.

Outlook of Occupation—Chances of employment, of advancing in the field or related fields. Permanency of occupation.

Student's Personal Appraisal of Job—Why he might or might not like it. How he feels he is suited for it. His limitations.

Whereas one could spend many more sessions on this phase, it is advisable not to try the patience of the class too far. Again, I point out the immaturity of the group. To them, senior year is very far away. Many will do the job well, many grudgingly, some might as well not have started. We're not all master teachers, you know (present company excepted). If one finds he is not successful in selling the unit, it should be dropped. If we can't do it well, it's better not to prejudice the youngsters against the guidance program. May I point out that the success of this unit depends upon the *availability of enough occupational material* to go around the class. An *Occupational Outlook Handbook* for each student would be ideal but a little expensive.

The survey will provide time for the counselor to visit with each student and discuss his ideas on careers and school. This is a good chance to get to know them better.

Week 14. Introduction of course planning and the idea of "what he can do—not what career he wants." Explanation of high school course of studies, required courses, point system for graduation. Description of courses when necessary.

Week 15. Begin individual program planning. Discussions of mimeographed information material. Question and answer session. Explanation of daily schedule.

Weeks 16, 17, 18. Individual programming. The students work out tentative programs. The counselor confers with each to make suggestions. A copy of the approved schedule is sent home for parents' approval and signature.

This phase offers another opportunity for individual guidance, some of which should be followed up by a private conference in the guidance office. There is an advantage to having all the youngsters in one room where they are easy to reach. There is the disadvantage though of discussing certain problems of planning within earshot of the group.

As soon as a student has made out an approved program, he can be rescheduled for a study hall rather than waste his time in the guidance class.

This group guidance course is a difficult trick to pull off successfully. I know it can be done. We've done it in our school with only moderate success. However, our weakness was lack of adequate source materials.

The most challenging part of the course is, of course, the unit on occupational information. The problem here is to maintain interest in an age group that is really not as interested in guidance as we are. It is necessary to discuss families of occupations in which the individual student has no interest whatsoever. And, as I've mentioned before, since the course usually lacks credit toward graduation, it also lacks authority. Maybe such credit should be given although I find it hard to justify this and would find it difficult to determine a basis for evaluating a student's efforts were credit given.

Nevertheless, I feel strongly that if one is a good teacher and has the necessary resource material, it *can* succeed. In our school, the course was taught before the innovation of modern technological advances in teaching techniques. An imaginative teacher, using modern gadgetry, should be able to develop an effective course. Certainly, some phases of the course such as individual

programming and career planning could well be incorporated
into an abbreviated group guidance program with considerable
saving of time as a result. I would encourage the beginning counselor to experiment in the expectation of coming up with a program that works for him.

Other forms of group activity

If a group guidance class is considered unwise or is impossible
to schedule, a series of assemblies can serve a useful function.
An assembly program has the disadvantage of being impersonal,
a one-way communication, and is unwieldy because of the size
of the audience. It is a time-saver, however. May I suggest the
following assemblies which we have found useful. I have organized them for a four-year high school.

Early September. Orientation for Freshmen. Welcome by Student Council President. Members of various extra-curricula activities give brief description of their organizations and invite
membership.

September. Meeting of all college and school bound seniors.
Discussion of school choice, multiple application, mechanics and
timing of admission, college boards and scholarship application.
Invite early guidance conference.

September. Meeting of all seniors intending to go on to work.
Explanation of placement service. Brief dissertation concerning
competition for jobs, teacher recommendations and similar thinly
veiled threats. Include a bit on the responsibility to employer.
(Usually a very boring session for all. Good idea to have some
humorous anecdotes on hand.)

September. Meeting of all college and school bound juniors. Pep
talk on importance of junior year punctuated by stifled yawns.
Explanation of PSAT in October. Emphasize advisability of SAT
in spring. Brief exposition of scholarship aid—qualifications and
sources. Explanation of National Merit Scholarship Qualifying
Test.

Early October. Short meeting for juniors to brief them on PSAT.
Details of seating, nature and purpose of test (a repeat). Techniques of taking tests. Reminder to bring fee and read informa-
tional booklet. Pass out booklets.

February. Meeting with college and school bound seniors. Discuss local scholarship programs. Pass out mimeographed materials.

March-April. Series of assemblies featuring military obligation. The initial meeting will include a complete explanation of various programs of the services with advantages and disadvantages. Current policy of draft (if they've decided what it is). Speakers from various branches of the armed forces.

Use of homerooms

I don't believe in the idea of teachers doing work that is the responsibility of the counselor. I agree that many would do an excellent guidance job, but they have enough to do as it is. However, homeroom periods are convenient times for the counselor to brief students on routine matters such as review of courses prior to registration for upperclassmen, or visiting with freshmen during the opening weeks of school to determine errors or any difficulties they may be having in classes. Conferences can be scheduled on the spot.

Other group activities

When our school was smaller and housed the freshmen, we used to visit the eighth graders in the various schools that sent us students. At this time a complete description of the freshmen course of studies was offered. The daily routine was explained along with the point system and requirements for graduation. In June we invited these groups to visit the high school for a morning. Student Council members took small groups on a tour of the building and we ended up with a question and answer period. We think this kind of orientation was helpful for the more apprehensive kids. Change of schools is quite an adventure to them.

These activities, plus the career day and field trips to industry previously mentioned, comprise the chief group activities that seem to have had value for our school. Notice that all these activities are primarily devices for imparting information.

If the time and space are available, voluntary group conferences on occupations could be worthwhile if well worked out in advance. They provide a medium for group discussion of the elements of job choice included above and particularly for such intangibles as job satisfaction, life values, etc. This might be done with Tri-Hi-Y and Hi-Y groups as well. Ideally, however, it should be available to all students. A similar series of conferences could be held on school and college choice.

A group therapy experiment

Some years ago we had an opportunity to organize a small group therapy class under the leadership of a psychiatrist from a nearby hospital who at that time was working with the local juvenile court. Several of our girls were involved in a variety of minor offenses and, through the Probation Office, the high school guidance staff and school nurse became involved.

A series of weekly meetings were set up in the court chambers. This plan proved to be as successful as any such group session probably could be. In the first place, it was conducted and directed by the psychiatrist who was a very warm, experienced, and intelligent woman. The counselors had no part in the discussions —but followed up each session with informal individual counseling which usually consisted of little more than a casual discussion of what happened that day and the girl's reaction to it.

Secondly, the group was remarkably homogeneous in the type of home background, level of intelligence, and even to the type of emotional problems involved. All the girls were either from broken homes or from homes where one or both parents drank to excess. In all cases, the girls felt rejected and insecure.

Therapy took the form of a Rogerian-oriented general discussion where attitudes were defined, challenged, compared and, in a few cases, significantly changed by the girls. I don't know the details of the methods the doctor used. I only know that in this case, under the most favorable conditions, she helped three of the five girls without question. Four of the five girls graduated. Three are happily married and appear well adjusted. A fourth girl is in the process of her third divorce. We have lost track of the fifth girl who never finished school.

To what degree the therapy alone helped is hard to evaluate. I don't discount the effect that the interest shown by the court and the school might have had in building up a trust in authority and society.

The important point is that here is an example of group therapy as I think it should be done—by a skilled professional working with a small group of youngsters with similar backgrounds and problems. While I deplore the prospect of counselors acting the psychiatrist, I'm aware of the need for expanded psychiatric school services and the possibilities of group therapy. If the *right person* is available, I urge that programs similar to what I have described be tried in your school. Unfortunately, psychiatrists and clinical psychologists are in such demand these days, it is most difficult to secure their services.

Summary

Group guidance activities offer an opportunity to the busy counselor to impart information to large groups at one time and thus become time-saving devices. At their best, these activities may also provide a valuable vehicle for stimulating group discussion—the element missing from individual conferences. But all group activity must be well planned and implemented. A unit in occupations can be effective if the leader is a skilled teacher and the resource material is adequate for a large group. I have suggested an outline for such a course but would expect the counselor to change it according to his particular needs and the circumstances. I have also suggested some of the difficulties and dangers in attempting such a unit.

I believe that an eclectic approach is best for the counselor. I urge him to try those things he thinks he can do and which promise the greatest success. However, all approaches to occupational information should be designed to expand rather than to limit the student's choice. Early job interest should be considered as temporary. The youngster should be encouraged to keep an open mind and wait as long as possible before committing himself. We should recognize the fact that career choice is a complicated, highly personal decision, one that is a continuous process spanning several years and involving many elements. Finally, I urge the counselor to emphasize life values and the intangible rewards that are such an important part of a career choice.

Bibliography

California Interest Inventory—California Test Bureau. Los Angeles, California.

Kuder Preference Record—Personal–Form A and Vocational–Form C. Science Research Associates, Inc., Chicago, Illinois.

S.R.A. Youth Inventory Form A—Science Research Associates, Inc., Chicago, Illinois.

See the bibliography for Chapter 7 for reference material on occupational information.

9

Organizing the Guidance Staff
Within a School System

Who's Who Around Here?

It is quite true that the work of the guidance counselor defies description. I am often asked "What *is* Guidance?" at social occasions. At this point I have found it convenient to spill my drink down the nearest décolletage and escape in the confusion.

Because our job is amorphous, difficult to describe and subject to misinterpretation, it becomes all the more important that the role of the counselor and everyone connected with pupil personnel services be carefully defined. It is also true that whenever there are two or more individuals engaged in a task, one should boss.

This chapter will deal with the organization of a typical guidance program and the deployment of counselors within a school.

Lines of command and staff function

In any school system, the top brass is the superintendent. He has the authority over and responsibility for the entire system. He delegates authority to the school principals who, in turn, have a similar responsibility and authority within their own buildings. In a large system, there is also a guidance director—sometimes called a director of pupil personnel services—who works directly under the superintendent in a staff capacity. His job is to supervise and coordinate the professional services provided by counselors and other members of the pupil personnel services team. He acts as advisor to the school principal. The counselors themselves are under the direct authority of the principal. He, in turn, cooperates with the guidance director in the operation of guidance services while retaining the ultimate authority over the guidance staff within his building. Finally, there may be other specialists in guidance-related services, such as school psychologists, social workers, etc., who work under the director of guidance.

The following is a diagram showing the lines of command and staff in a typical guidance organization. (This brings back happy memories of Army days!) Lines of command denote responsibility for and authority over the subordinate personnel. Lines of staff indicate an advisory or supervisory function and indicate a co-operative rather than authoritative relationship.

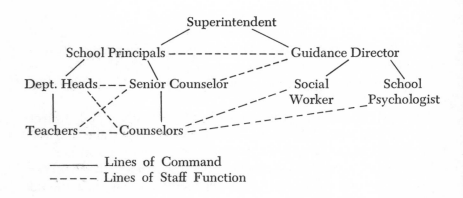

If the system employs a city-wide guidance director as in the diagram above, it is advisable to have a senior counselor in each building with the authority and duties comparable to a depart-ment head. In a smaller system, the guidance director may be the senior counselor who operates with a reduced pupil load. In this case, he usually works more directly with the school principal and less directly with the superintendent.

I should point out here that, although the diagram does not clearly indicate it, counselors should deal directly with department heads in matters concerning policies or problems involving his department. In the case of individual pupil problems, we would go directly to the teachers concerned, of course.

Should counselors be specialists?

Within a high school, the guidance staff may be deployed in several ways. There are four fairly common schemes in operation.

PLAN 1

COUNSELOR A	COUNSELOR B	COUNSELOR C	
General Pupils	Commercial Pupils	College Pupils	*Senior Class*
General Pupils	Commercial Pupils	College Pupils	*Junior Class*
General Pupils	Commercial Pupils	College Pupils	*Sophomore Class*
General Pupils	Commercial Pupils	College Pupils	*Freshman Class*

In Plan 1, the assignment of counselors to students is based on the vocational or educational objectives of the pupil. One counselor will counsel all those pupils in the college course from grade nine through twelve. Another will counsel the commercial course students. A third will be assigned the general or vocational students. Each counselor will follow his counselees through to graduation. Each counselor is responsible for placement within his field.

Under this plan, counselors become specialists and are able to devote their time to a particular area—presumably in more depth than in an unspecialized scheme. This plan is more common in large schools or in schools where the particular backgrounds of counselors lend themselves naturally to this specialization.

On paper it looks good. My criticism is aimed at the assumption that it is possible to determine vocational choice and educational goals in the ninth grade. I maintain this is a delusion. Such a plan reflects a rigidity of school and guidance philosophy. It necessitates a compartmentalized and inflexible curriculum. Within the flexible curriculum which I advocate, it would be difficult to label a student as General, Business or strictly College in many cases. A specialized guidance program makes the movement of students from one course curriculum to another—from business to college course, for instance—very difficult. They have already been categorized and placed in compartments. What's worse, the counselor has been sealed in the same compartment. In other words, this plan is in opposition to the whole philosophy expressed in this book.

PLAN 2

COUNSELOR A		*Senior Class*
COUNSELOR B		*Junior Class*
COUNSELOR C		*Sophomore Class*
COUNSELOR D		*Freshman Class*

In Plan 2, each counselor is assigned a class—or portion of a class—and follows it through to graduation whereupon he picks up the following class of incoming freshmen.

This is an unspecialized plan. Each counselor is responsible for educational and vocational counseling and placement for his group. It allows him to get to know his counselees extremely well before they reach the decision-making senior year.

However, in the senior year the counselor is really overburdened. There is so much activity and work necessary for school and job placement that a counselor with the responsibility of an entire class may not have the time to do the job properly. Furthermore, a certain amount of continuity in the area of placement, including contact with schools and employers, is lost when a counselor is engaged in these activities only once every four years.

These are not insurmountable obstacles, but they are problems which should be considered.

PLAN 3

In this plan, each counselor is assigned to a class as in Plan 2, but the difference here is that the freshman class counselor will pick up the next freshman class each year, while the sophomore class counselor inherits the freshman class, and so on. The freshman class counselor counsels *only* freshmen and *always* freshmen. He is the *freshman* counselor. The other counselors are likewise either sophomore, junior or senior class counselors—always the same class.

As far as I am concerned, there is nothing to recommend this plan. The most obvious weakness is that each counselor has the same group of students for just one year, sacrificing any real possibility of getting to know the kids at all!

PLAN 4

COUNSELOR A	COUNSELOR B	COUNSELOR C	COUNSELOR D	
				Senior Class
				Junior Class
				Sophomore Class
				Freshman Class

I believe Plan 4 to be the most effective utilization of counselors. In this, the student body is divided vertically by alphabet and each counselor is assigned a portion of each class. He keeps his portion of each class through graduation and is responsible for job and school placement for his assigned seniors.

This plan has the advantage of dividing the load equally. It allows for knowledge of students, since the counselor has them for four years. It reflects the philosophy of a flexible curriculum, since the students are not divided by type of course or vocational objective. It permits the counselor to participate in all phases of guidance activities—a far more stimulating and satisfying job experience than any narrow specialization can provide.

Of course, this plan necessitates well-rounded and experienced counselors. However, over the years I have watched several new counselors assume these responsibilities and acquire the knowledge necessary to implement this method of counselor use. I know that any good counselor can develop into a successful expert in job and school placement. It takes time, to be sure, but it is worth waiting for.

There is another type of specialization which is gradually gaining favor (although not with me). In this system, counselors are given the usual counseling load based on a vertical split as in Plan 4. However, they are specialists in placement activities. One counselor will have *all* the college placement—his own counselees and those of the other counselors as well. Another counselor will be in charge of job placement of all those students who are in the job market. A third counselor may have all the testing as his specialty and so on.

To me, this is giving up, in the senior year, all the rapport and pupil knowledge built up over the preceding years. How could anyone successfully counsel a complete stranger on college admissions? By successfully, I mean arriving at a school choice based on the student's interests, abilities, personality and his financial situation, to mention just a few factors that influence school choice.

To be sure, the student's own counselor could supply this information, but this would be a time-consuming duplication of effort. The same criticism holds with job placement or any post-high school planning. Furthermore, at times of crucial decision, a high degree of rapport is necessary if the counselor is to be of real assistance to the pupil. Counseling strangers is just not feasible.

Sometimes this kind of specialization develops from outside pressures; particularly when an experienced counselor is working with a staff of neophytes. Here the temptation is strong to let the experienced counselor take over the responsibility for those functions that lie in sensitive areas. I refer to college placement, for example. In many communities, the school is evaluated by the citizenry according to its college placement record. You and I know better, but such are the times. None the less, I urge administrators to resist the pressure and allow the inexperienced counselor to engage in college placement and all the activities normal in counseling seniors. The inexperienced counselors will learn rapidly and, under the supervision of the old hands, develop into valuable, all-around counselors.

Limited Specialization

At the same time, I would enthusiastically endorse the practice of giving a counselor the responsibility for coordinating a guidance function. In our school, one counselor has the responsibility for coordinating school and college placement. He sets up conferences with visiting admissions officers, for instance. But all counselors meet with these school representatives to be informed. This same counselor visits colleges, but all counselors are briefed as to what he observes. Each counselor counsels his own pupils on school choice. The coordinator keeps the other counselors informed and attempts to see that *all* the students are not pointed towards the same college. Of course, the final choice is the student's but a certain amount of guidance—call it influence if you wish—should be supplied by the counselor to avoid excessive competition within the school.

In a similar fashion, another counselor coordinates job placement, although each counselor advises his own counselees. In this case, the placement counselor often makes the initial contact with a prospective employer and is briefed by both the student's counselor and any appropriate teacher if the job entails classroom training. So, to a degree, the placement counselor is a specialist, but only in that most job requests are channeled through the placement service. Each individual counselor still has the responsibility for job counseling and placement for his counselees. The coordinating counselor handles the machinery of getting student and employer together and keeps the placement records, and, of course, he has a normal load of counselees for whom he is responsible in all phases of guidance.

We also have a counselor who coordinates the testing program, sets up dates, procures testing material, etc. But all the counselors assist in the testing and do the interpretations themselves.

The fourth member of the staff has the responsibility of compiling records and reports, such as the follow-up, academic inventory, compilations of test results, questionnaires, etc. Each of the other counselors supplies him with the information necessary for the compilation.

And so, while each counselor has an area of responsibility, each is actively involved with his counselees in every phase of guidance. The result, I like to believe, is a highly *personal program* based on the counselor's close relationship with his youngster. Anything less loses the whole point of guidance and is a step nearer to counseling by computers.

Sex and the Counselor

This spicy paragraph heading is unfortunately misleading, as the reader will soon discover.

In the early days of my career, we had a woman counselor for the girls and I was the boys' counselor. We were smaller then and I went along for years not realizing what I was missing. When the time came to add more counselors, we each took a class and followed it through to graduation. When we changed to a 3–3 system, we were faced with the prospect of four counselors for three classes, so we split the school vertically into four slices and we each took our alphabetical share of each of the three classes. This system has persisted until today.

I confess that I had some misgivings about my role as counselor to girls. After ten years of working with only boys, plus my traumatic experience of rearing a teen-age daughter, I doubted both my ability to relate successfully to the weaker sex and my willingness to subject myself to the ordeal. Time has proven my doubts unfounded.

I have found—together with my male colleague—that girls generally relate better to men than to women counselors. And, to my chagrin, I feel that boys accept the counsel of women counselors as readily and, in some cases, more completely than that of men counselors.

In the first case, I feel we men provide a kind of father image to girls—a father, however, that is no threat to them and who is far more approachable than their own father. I refer again to that well-known characteristic of the teen-ager who finds it so difficult to communicate with either parent much as he may love them. Our part in the lives of students is transitory, strictly part time. Kids, realizing this, find it easier to open up to a sympathetic male who does not represent authority.

Boys, on the other hand, are less apt to reveal a weakness to another male. It is unmanly to do so. I have seen only half a dozen boys in tears in twenty years of guidance. Girls cry at the drop of a Kleenex. They positively enjoy crying in front of a male, and I must confess I react positively with a surge of sympathetic, manly consolation. Just what they are looking for!

So if the reader is contemplating a similar organization of the guidance staff, rest assured that a coeducational split works well, although I'm not ready to accept an all-girl group of counselees at this writing. Of course, I'm becoming feeble, and probably foolish, in my middle age.

Coordination and communications

There is an urgent need for a coordinated team approach to guidance. It is easy for the counselor to become so involved in his own students' problems that he ignores the rest of the program. In an unspecialized guidance setup, this can weaken the overall effectiveness of the total program by fostering confusion and a duplication of effort. A constant exchange of information and ideas between counselors, administration and faculty is essential to efficient operation.

I'm against useless meetings and committees. But a weekly meeting of the high school counseling staff and administration is valuable. Such formal meetings provide a means for constantly evaluating the program. The city guidance director should sit in on these frequently. For me, these are highly enjoyable breaks from the routine, featuring coffee, stories of questionable propriety and a lively exchange of information and opinion.

All communications and mail of interest to the whole staff is routed from one counselor to the next to return to the secretary for filing or appropriate action.

The city guidance director should hold monthly meetings with the guidance staffs of the junior and senior high schools in order to effect a coordinated program. Since the junior high counselors initiate the important choice of individual programs in high school, they should be thoroughly informed as to curriculum or policy changes. After all, the high school counselors are the ones who can best evaluate the junior high guidance program in so far as it relates to pupil performance in high school.

This evaluation should be undertaken with tact and forbearance. But if we find, in the high school for example, that too many eighth grade students are electing high school courses beyond their capacity, it is our duty to inform our junior high colleagues. After all, how can they know these things unless we tell them! Obviously, it is in situations like this that a mutual respect and trust between the two staffs is so important. Needless to say, the guidance director acts as referee and mediator, interposing his body between combatants with complete indifference to his own safety.

It is assumed that the guidance director will keep the superintendent informed. To this end, I suggest that a written guidance philosophy and job description for all guidance personnel be submitted to the superintendent for his information and approval. I would hope that he would forward copies of each to the members of the school board in the interest of better understanding of the guidance function—a function badly misunderstood by most laymen.

Summary

How a guidance program is organized depends on the particular school situation and the needs of the student body. I have outlined some guidelines that seem important to me. Responsibilities and authority should be defined. Lines of communications must be kept active and extensive. The plan for utilization of guidance personnel may reflect the characteristics of a school. But certain elements should be present in any such plan of deployment. Most important is that the counselor keep the same students throughout high school. Secondly, the plan should not encourage the premature assignment of students to any fixed category, such as college, noncollege, business, vocational and the like. Finally, the plan which is most likely to effect the successful utilization of counselors is the one which provides the most flexibility for the student in his educational development.

10

How to Get the Teacher's Active Support

The Uneasy Truce

Teachers don't really hate counselors, although many may take a dim view of us. It is not hard to understand. Teachers have a different and more limited view of the academic scene—and quite properly so. As a group, they are interested in their subjects and in standards. They are concerned with performance and achievement. They usually do not have the time to search into the background and psyches of their students to diagnose the reasons for underachievement or an unwillingness to conform.

This is not to say that teachers are uninterested in individuals. Of course they are—at least good teachers are. I have already pointed out that much valuable guidance is carried on by administrators, teachers and coaches. But these people don't have the time to research and counsel every student. Generally, they are concerned with classroom performance first and as it is evidenced in their own classroom. They are not too concerned with the performance of the student in other areas—or if they are, it is a secondary interest.

Let me expound further. I have never met a good Latin teacher that didn't think Latin was the most important subject in the school. To our geometry teacher, the Pythagorean theorem is the most significant statement since Moses received the Ten Commandments. Our chemistry teacher holds to the unswerving opinion that anyone without acid burns on his sweater is some kind of Neanderthal nut and obviously belongs in a special class for defectives. And so it goes.

At the same time, I would be dishonest not to admit that at one time or another each of these teachers has helped certain students far more than I was able to. But the fact is that teachers usually do not have the time nor the knowledge of the total background of students to be consistently engaged in guidance activities. If they did, I would still be a teacher.

Guidance counselors, on the other hand, are not personally involved in the arena of the classroom and can afford to view the scene with dispassionate detachment. They are in a position to see the whole picture and appreciate the fact that, for Joe, football might be more important than French 3 to his growth in self-confidence and, consequently, to his ultimate academic success. Yet if I agreed to let Joe drop French—floundering badly as he was—in order to give him more time for his other subjects and football too, his teacher would never really agree with the wisdom of the move, no matter how skillfully I pleaded my case. And if I were the teacher, I'd probably feel the same way.

Realizing this difference in the attitude of the teacher and counselor is basic to good counselor-teacher relations. The counselor is bound to offend faculty sensibilities at times, but he can avoid much grief by respecting the teacher's point of view. This is one reason why I believe a counselor should have first been a classroom teacher. Only then can he appreciate the teacher's feelings and attitudes.

I have stated before that the function of guidance should be to reinforce, no matter how indirectly, the efforts of the classroom teacher. What goes on in the classroom is the reason for schools. And so, it behooves us to view the classroom as a very special sanctuary and the teacher as its high Lama.

Probably the most common and most heinous crime committed by counselors is that of interrupting the teacher in the middle of a teaching session. This breach of etiquette is bound to bring down the wrath of a righteously indignant colleague. If carried to excess, it alone can force an irremediable rift between faculty and guidance. I still make this mistake, but usually I evaluate the situation carefully before I decide it's important enough to disrupt the flow of classroom activity. Even then, I interrupt on bended knee and, if occasion permits, extend a brief word of explanation to calm ruffled feeings. (I indulge in hyperbole for the sake of emphasis—not that I feel teachers are genetically hypersensitive or without understanding themselves.)

Counselors are not the only ones who are conscious of the ticking clock; teacher time is valuable, too. The counselor should be sure that when he removes a student or a group of students from class, it is with adequate reason. Pupil interviews should be scheduled before or after school and during study halls. In our school, we use Saturdays for PSAT and National Merit Testing. We try to give teachers prior notice if we take a student out to visit with a school representative. We leave the student in class if a test or very important class activity is scheduled for that day.

But try as we may, there are always too many occasions when a student is missing from a class—no matter how justified it may seem to us. And so, in this respect at least, a certain amount of criticism, no matter how amiable, is levied at the guidance office.

Helping the teacher understand the guidance viewpoint

All of the annoyances mentioned above can be borne stoically, however, if the faculty understands the purpose and function of guidance as it relates to these various affronts. I advocate one faculty meeting a year to discuss problems of procedure and policy as it relates to the classroom and curriculum in general. These often develop into a lively give and take, but guidance counselors have thick skins and usually survive. Such open discussions do much to clear the air and clarify motives and reasons for guidance activities.

I also advise an annual orientation session with all new teachers where the guidance program is explained and the message "What can we do to *help* you?" rings out loud and clear.

All too often, information is collected and compiled by the guidance staff only to remain in the guidance office. Much of this is of interest to teachers and, if made available to them, would increase their understanding of the guidance program and of their pupils.

Teachers should receive copies of the one- and five-year follow-up compilations. These would provide them with a picture of what is happening to their students. Teachers, of all people, should see the report on their products. It is surprising to me that more teachers do not ask what Mary or Sam are doing a year or two after graduation. I'm sure they are interested. I'm not sure they realize that we have this information.

For the same reasons we supply the ninth grade teachers in junior high school with a copy of the first semester sophomore grades for their information.

The results of group testing should reach the faculty in one form or another. The low reading ability of a student is a particularly significant bit of information of interest to his teachers. Indeed, high or low scores in any aptitude or skill are matters of concern to the classroom teacher who is continually evaluating the pupil's ability, industry and motivation.

Similarly, college board results, particularly achievement test results, should be given to teachers who use them in evaluating their own classroom effectiveness in relation to individuals.

Most colleges send a mid-year academic report back to the student's secondary school. These can be made available to teachers as another rough evaluation of the school's product, in the area of college preparation, at least.

Of course, all these reports take time to reproduce in quantity. May I digress at this point and urge that some kind of photocopier be a standard piece of guidance equipment. It will more than justify its considerable cost by reproducing, in a matter of minutes, reports, transcripts of grades, reprints, etc.

How to bring the teacher into the guidance program

Aside from the obvious benefit to the jobs of both teacher and counselor, the exchange of information and opinion on students is an effective method of increasing faculty acceptance of guidance. Everyone likes to be asked his opinion. However, the main reason for this exchange is more significant than mere guidance acceptance by the faculty. It is an important function of guidance to inform teachers of the problems, background and interests of their students to the end that more effective learning will take place. Often, a teacher will be able to produce new information and insights that will be useful to the counselor. This kind of co-operation marks the ideal teacher-counselor relationship. It is not rare, but it is unfortunate that it is not universal.

Teachers can be used to implement the guidance program in more formal, planned ways. Since they have an enthusiasm for their subject and are education oriented, teachers are in a good position to practice a little vocational and educational guidance and usually welcome the opportunity.

Because of their nature, certain classes, particularly those with a vocational function, lend themselves well to a teacher-conducted session on vocational and educational opportunities stemming from the course.

For example, the drafting (mechanical drawing) teacher should be supplied with up-to-date occupational materials on drafting, tool and machine design together with catalogs and other descriptive material of technical and engineering schools—particularly those in the immediate area. If it is possible to combine this unit with a visit to a plant in order to see the draftsman, designer and engineer in action, the impact is even greater.

Similar material can be supplied to the shop teachers. I have already described the field trips that have been a part of our industrial arts program.

Art, music, foods, clothing, bookkeeping, stenography, biology, chemistry and physics teachers should be supplied with appropriate vocational and educational information to be integrated into the regular course. Even the humanities can serve a similar function with the use of some imagination.

It is not hard to sell this idea to teachers. I suggest letting the teachers choose their own way of presenting the materials. Encourage them to suggest additional materials they would like.

I'm convinced that this approach can be more effective in the hands of *willing* teachers than if attempted in the guidance office. The material has a timeliness, an authority and a purpose that might not exist to such a degree outside the classroom.

I would like to see a unit in the senior Problems of Democracy (or its parallel) course which examines education in the U.S.—its history, current philosophy and purpose. I would hope for a lively debate on the value of training as opposed to education and a thorough exposition of the significance of the liberal arts in a modern society. Such a unit would relieve the counselor of the necessity for spelling out some of the reasons for going on to higher education.

Of course, one can't do this all in one year but once initiated, the program becomes self-perpetuating with each teacher.

I came to a tardy realization of the possibilities of faculty guidance some years ago when I invited our mechanical drawing teacher to accompany me to an open house for counselors at a nearby mechanical design technology school. He became a part of the guidance program at that point. I urge counselors to invite appropriate members of the faculty on similar school and college visits.

I was most gratified when our chemistry teacher recently arranged with us a conference between the science-oriented students and a visiting professor of a college where the teacher had been taking summer institute courses. This is the kind of voluntary faculty participation that pays off in big dividends.

There is another broad area in which the counselor can enlist faculty participation—that of attitude formation. I don't believe that attitudes can be taught directly to a class of teenagers. But attitudes can be developed indirectly by the dissemination of accurate information and through open discussion.

The counselor is particularly sensitive to the presence or absence of good value formation, since many of his problems stem from their lack. He is also in a position to evaluate the overall tone of his school and the subtle changes in attitudes of the student body as the youngsters react to the social scene. He also receives much professional literature that deals with the problems of current adolescent values. So, from time to time, it may be possible for him to approach his principal with an idea for a faculty attack on a problem.

What, for example, is your school doing about the problems of drug abuse? Of premarital sex relations? Of teen-age drinking? These are problems which unfortunately intrude on the high school scene all too often these days. They are problems which lend themselves to a unit in social studies, English or biology. If the students do the research and compile the information under the direction of the instructor, the blight of adult authority is removed and the material becomes acceptable in the eyes of the youngsters. Frank discussions will further the process of attitude formation. At no time should the teacher force an opinion on or prejudge the problem. Of course, he can state his own opinions for consideration, discussion and challenge.

The formation and implementation of such units is the responsibility of the principal working with the department heads and teachers. But the counselor can initiate and push the idea.

In a similar vein, why not attack the problem of marks? We all deplore the tendency of kids to look upon grades as an end in themselves. Why not introduce some experiments in grading systems in order to put the emphasis back on learning, where it belongs? How about a pass-fail semester (a system recently adopted by many colleges)? Or no marks at all in other courses for a semester? Several interesting lessons in human nature might be revealed. It certainly would put the pressure on a teacher to motivate a class for which the rewards and punishments of grades had been removed. Would your faculty be willing to try something like this? How about a course where there were no assignments? Students would work on a subject of their own choice for a semester. No classes, no grades, just the advice and guidance of a faculty member and a pass or fail at the conclusion of the course. It could be called a "Tutorial Course" and should appeal to the imaginative youngster who would take it as an elective.

Of course, I believe in the idea of competition and have nothing against an evaluation of a pupil's work. It is part of training for a competitive world. But it is refreshing to depart from the traditional at times, and especially when the tradition is dragging in a dusty rut.

The point is that a counselor is more aware of the tyranny of grades than anyone and has this opportunity to "needle" his principal into initiating programs that will bring matters into a new and proper perspective.

As with any attempt to innovate, a good working relationship between faculty, principal and counselor is a prerequisite. The counselor can only suggest ideas and provide useful information for administrative consideration. However, school curricula have a habit of remaining static, and there is no one better positioned than the counselor to stir up the academic pudding.

It is perhaps unfair of me to imply that your principal has not already introduced similar programs. But administrators are too often bogged down in details. It remains for us to jolt them from time to time into positive action. The kinds of teacher activities I have described are either matters of policy involving administrative approval or are areas of teaching techniques. In the first case, the counselor has no authority to initiate the programs; and in the second, he should not have the temerity to suggest to teachers how they should teach. So we must convince the principal to use his influence and authority to promote a cooperative and imaginative faculty attack on these and other issues that come to our attention by virtue of our peculiar position. I refer, of course, to the fact that even while sitting, the counselor has an ear to the ground.

A compendium of teacher complaints

Over the years I have accumulated as fine a collection of teachers' gripes about guidance as anyone in the business. Indeed, if there is any field in which I consider myself an expert, it is in my knowledge of faculty complaints. I come by this knowledge honestly since most of these criticisms were aimed at me, and often were well deserved. It is a wise man that learns from another's folly, however, and so I will pass a small part of my collection along to you, the reader.

Gripe 1: "Guidance counselors take the part of the student against the teacher." Well, of this, at least, I'm not guilty. Maybe once or twice in the past in my more quixotic days, but no more. Guidance is supposed to be a "soft" process. But sometimes, in our role of listener rather than judge, we may give the impression that we are espousing the cause of the pupil in cases of teacher-pupil clashes. Part of our job is to interpret the teacher and his actions to the pupil so that the student will accept both—even though he may disagree. I urge the counselor to ignore the question of who is right or wrong in circumstances like these and concentrate on the problem of helping the student accept and adjust to the situation. If conditions warrant it, the counselor should acquaint the teacher involved with the gist of his remarks to the student in order to avoid any misinterpretation. If the counselor feels the youngster is getting a bad deal (and the case is serious enough), he should refer it to the principal. But as a general rule, never criticize a teacher in front of a pupil or in anyway undermine the teacher's authority or personal stature. On the other hand, as I have previously indicated, there is nothing wrong in pointing out a student's mistakes in reacting to the problem.

To look at a common example, take the case of Jack, a real swinger and, as we educators say, highly verbal. (That's educational jargon meaning he had a big mouth.) The scene is the auditorium study hall and for once Jack is deeply engrossed in homework he should have done the night before. Miss K., a new teacher, is presiding. There is a commotion in the general area around Jack and, before you can say John Dewey, he (Jack not John) finds himself saddled with two hours of detention. Jack is momentarily dumbstruck, then rallies and, with righteous indignation, stoutly and loudly protests his innocence. Miss K. stands firm, though her knees are shaking. Jack persists in his defense and receives another hour for his troubles. This stops him and fortunately so because, by this time, Miss K. is a little panicky. Jack spends the rest of the period seething and then bursts into my office where he pours out his tale of woe.

So we have a case where, if I am to believe Jack (and I do), the student is the victim of a teacher mistake. My procedure is as follows:

1. Let Jack talk himself out.
2. Give him a lifesaver. (He has burned up considerable energy at this point.)
3. Ask him if he argued with the teacher. (I already have deduced this.)
4. Point out error #1. One must never argue with a teacher in front of a class. This challenges her authority and puts the teacher in an impossible position as far as a negotiated peace is concerned.
5. I ask him, with a straight face, whether he has ever "gotten away with anything" in this study hall before. Jack, being realistic (he knows I know him), admits to one or two minor infractions.

6. I point out to him that he was lucky then and anyone's luck is bound to change if he plays the ponies long enough.
7. I elaborate on Miss K.'s position which is, indeed, the position of any teacher. She must call the shots as she sees them, and Jack's reputation contributed to her honest error. I add a few words about the necessity of an authoritarian structure in a school.
8. I ask Jack if he has any important reason why he cannot serve the detention. He answers in the negative. I point out that either he must accept the detention or, to avoid further trouble, he must plead his case to the principal. Is it really that important to him? I get a negative grunt.
9. At this point, I clap him heartily on the shoulder, give him another lifesaver and send him on his way—a sadder and maybe a wiser boy. (I like Jack.)

I'll bet this situation comes up a dozen times a year. Not all kids are as easy to talk to as Jack. He trusts me, or maybe it's the lifesavers that appeal to him. The fact is that teachers are human and are as prone to error and poor judgment as any of us. It is up to the counselor to help his counselees accept this reality and adjust to all kinds of people and a variety of demands.

Gripe 2: "You counselors have it pretty soft—no study halls, no lunch duty, no homeroom, no detention duty." The implied rebuke here, of course, is that counselors sit on their backsides all day doing virtually nothing of tangible worth while teachers slave over a hot blackboard from dawn to dusk. My reaction to this is that we counselors should lean over backwards in our attempts to assist teachers, to inform them of what we *are* doing and, in truth, to make good use of our time. To busy teachers, the sight of counselors goofing off is a source of understandable irritation. Goof off in private!

Gripe 3: "You're scheduling too many kids in my class who can't keep up with the work." In a flexible curriculum, there is a real danger of flooding a class with so many academic risks as to dilute the standards of the course. If the counselor hears this complaint very often, he should take notice. This goes back to our discussion on scheduling and course planning. It's important enough to bear repetition. It is very difficult to find the middle road between the rigid scheduling that will guarantee a class of highly talented youngsters and the liberal scheduling that encourages any student to elect a course regardless of his chances of success. It becomes a matter of what is a justifiable risk. There should be something in the record that points strongly to the student's ability to do the work in a course. Beyond that, it's up to the counselor's discretion. Here again, we have a responsibility to help the teacher, to promote high standards of scholarship and, at the same time, to follow a policy that will deny no youngster the opportunity to accept a challenge. As previously noted, it helps to inform the teacher who these academic risks are. Teachers should realize that we don't expect them to mark these students any differently from the others. The risks either should measure up to class standards or they fail. Even so, this is a real and constant problem.

Gripe 4: "You counselors spend all your time with the college kids. Why don't you do something for the general course students?" All too often this criticism is justified. Counselors often *do* spend more time for the college bound, especially in their senior year. Of course, the fact remains that there are more things that need to be done in the college placement process. However, the temptation is to do more for these kids than is good for them, while we spend less and less time with the general course students. As I have pointed out, counseling general course students on career planning is a difficult and—in terms of tangible results— an unrewarding task. Yet these kids should get a fair share of our time if we mean what we say in our philosophy. Indeed, to do the job right, they really need *more* of our time. The good students will make it in spite of us.

Gripe 5: "What's the idea of letting Bill drop my course?" If the counselor hears that one, there has been a serious breakdown of communications. No student should be removed from or placed in a class without first consulting the teacher. Beyond this, the question points out some of the difficulties in course adjustments. Some teachers try to get rid of the under-achievers or slow students as soon as possible. Others attempt to hold the youngsters' noses to the grindstone—sometimes for longer than is desirable. In either case, the counselor has the task of selling an idea to the teacher. On the one hand, he may persuade the teacher to let the slow student hang on a little longer, while arranging for extra help; on the other hand, he may have to convince the teacher that, under the circumstances, the student is better off dropping the course. This type of problem exists primarily with under-achievers.

Lest I sound as though the counselor has complete control of this kind of class adjustment, let me hastily point out that parents as well as students and teachers should be involved in these decisions.

Gripe 6: "Can't you get Bill to do some homework?" This question implies that the counselor is somehow failing in his job. It also reveals a lack of understanding on the part of the teacher. Let's get things straight. The responsibility for motivating pupils and for the enforcement of homework policies is the teacher's. As counselors, we must appreciate the difficulty of this and should become involved in the problem of motivating the indifferent, the immature and the discouraged. Sometimes we can help. But it is a common misconception among teachers that a guidance counselor assumes this responsibility, that it is a major part of his job. Someone should disillusion the teacher who has so misconstrued the function of a guidance program. And, as counselors, we should not allow this misconception to become an accepted fact. If we *do* accept the total responsibility for pupils' motivation and for their work habits, we run the risk of being unable to produce and, in consequence, of bringing the guidance program into disrepute.

Gripe 7: "Your socks don't match your tie." Ignore this. Or try wearing your red jacket with the brass buttons.

Oh yes, there are many others. But these will give you an idea of what we're up against. I've often remarked that I have no trouble with kids, just teachers. But, think of the cross *they* bear!

In self-defense, I've compiled my own list of complaints about teachers, although I've never had the courage to voice them. However, in case any teachers are eavesdropping on this dialogue (I love that expression!), I will list a few. It should do little to stifle the perennial teacher-counselor feud, but things have been getting rather dull here lately.

Gripe 1: "Why do teachers always consider a question about one of their students' grades as a personal attack on their professional competence?" This, of course, is a grossly unfair generalization. Yet every time I question a pupil's mark in an attempt to get information, I sense a distinct freeze. Teachers get really defensive about marks, or about discipline.

Gripe 2: "Why do so many teachers put such importance on fact memorization?" Yes, why do they? Granted that a background of significant facts is basic to a proper understanding, is it necessary to make the kids memorize every date, every English king, every order of insects, and forty-nine lines from Gray's "Elegy in a Country Church Yard"? Of course, this is a nonguidance area, but I have to counsel kids who are fed to the gills with a plethora of minutiae. And they have my sympathy. I claim this to be true of most traditional schools to a degree—and of many college courses. For some teachers (just a few), there will always be something sacred about the capitals of the fifty states, and you'd better learn them!

Gripe 3: "Why don't you teach your students how to study your course?" Many teachers do take time out for just this purpose. Others assume that kids know how to study. They don't! And I think that's why many won't.

Gripe 4: "When are you going to realize that your course is not as important to your kids as group acceptance, football and drive-ins?" Another generalization, of course. It is an unfortunate condition but true to a degree. It is such a help to teachers to assist in the extra-curricular activities of the youngsters—or, at least, to be aware and sympathetic with the little devils and the "adolescent syndrome." As a former teacher and current dispassionate observer, I have a theory that every teacher should be involved in some kind of extra-curricular activity for their own effectiveness. Of course, there are usually not that many activities to go around. But the theory still stands and, at the very least, any teacher can stop a boy in the hall and congratulate him on the twenty rebounds he made against Tech or compliment a girl on her striped purple stockings—roughly the equivalent.

I could go on and on (this is such fun), but I must restrain the impulse because, after all, I feel that we counselors transgress more than we are transgressed upon.

Conclusion

Most counselors have entered the academic scene in comparatively recent years and are, even now, looked upon with a degree of suspicion by the old-timers on the faculty. Because of a more limited set of objectives, teachers view the academic scene differently from counselors. Some look upon guidance as a sinecure. Some few see it only as a nuisance. The majority accept guidance as a necessary service, but most of these have their reservations about certain guidance philosophies and objectives.

The counselor should wage a constant battle to build a good working rapport with teachers. The guidance program should be planned to help teachers in as many ways as is possible. We should be teachers' aides and, as such, a part of the teaching team. Granted that we are concerned with the overall development of the child rather than with just an academic area; nevertheless, we should ally ourselves as closely as possible with the classroom. We should *not* be a separate entity working along a different track in our efforts to help the child towards a fruitful maturity, and we should never find ourselves in the position of *competing* with teachers for a student's time.

The strongest guidance program is the one that makes the best use of teacher time and talents. Many areas of the guidance program can be performed effectively in the classroom. If at all possible, teachers should be enlisted as *willing* assistants to the program—particularly in the areas of presenting information on occupational and educational opportunities.

Finally, since the counselor is in a favorable position to view the entire educational picture, he is in a position to innovate and initiate certain programs involving value formation on current adolescent problems. This is a kind of preventive approach where planned classroom activity may be more successful than a frontal attack by the counselor himself.

11

Anticipating the
Problems

Good Lord! What Next?

Up to now it might appear to
unwary eyes as though the guidance program, as depicted within
these covers, is tidily organized and neatly wrapped up. Unfortunately, in any guidance program, just when everything seems to
be progressing smoothly, all hell will break loose. Some red-eyed
kid is bound to appear and pour out a story of woe that would
make Oliver Twist look like a sweepstakes winner. If I sound impatient, my annoyance is occasioned not by the youngster, but
rather at the shortcomings of mankind, and in particular, at weak,
ignorant or genuinely sick parents. For, almost without fail, a real
problem child comes from a problem home.

Ours is a relatively favored community. We have neither the
problems of the very rich nor the despair of the ghetto. Yet in
this very "average" small city, we seem to have all the problems
that plague any community. I'm sure this is true throughout our
fair land.

As the pace of our American society increases, so apparently do the pressures that are reflected in neglected or rejected children. As we all know, we see these youngsters at a very sensitive age when, more than at any time in their life, they need the stability of a favorable home environment. They need the security of being loved, of belonging to a family united in mutual affection and respect. Deprived of this security, the youngster has the emotional rug pulled out from under him and trouble is bound to follow in varying degrees.

Not all the problems of the "unplanned program" stem from unfortunate home conditions. Many are inherent in the changes occasioned by the progressive stages of adolescence. During this period all problems are magnified in the minds of the youngsters, whether they be physical, social or psychological. Most of these are the expected, normal difficulties of the young, but they too engage the attention of the counselor. Finally, there are those unclassified problems that are the accidents of fate.

This chapter will deal with a variety of problems commonly encountered in a guidance office. Lest the reader anticipate solutions, may I readily admit that I have found relatively few. I will, however, suggest some avenues of attack as well as point out some of the pitfalls to avoid.

The under-achiever

Let's first consider a puzzling phenomenon which, although not in the category of real serious problems, has plagued parents and teachers for years.

By far the most frustrating problem the guidance counselor encounters, and with increasing frequency, is that of the youngster who apparently has adequate ability and training but who performs at a level much below that which might be expected of him. Such children try the patience of parents and teachers to the utmost limits since there seems to be no valid reason for their inability to achieve. Under-achievers with a secure, happy family background are as common as those from less fortunate homes.

While there seems to be no one answer to the problem, it is helpful to review the social scene as it has changed over the past 25 years in order to understand factors which appear to contribute to the phenomenon of the under-achiever.

In the first place, a greater emphasis is placed on the value of education today. Admittedly it is sometimes prized for the wrong reasons. Nevertheless, the pressures to succeed in school are growing each year. We see it in our school by the increase in number of freshmen who elect the college course, while the percentage of those who actually enter college—or who seem to have the scholastic ability for college—remains remarkably constant.

Add to this situation a breakdown of strong family ties, a deterioration of communications between parent and teen-ager, and a continuing policy of overpermissiveness. All these ingredients appear to stem from our present way of life—a life which is based on an increasing preoccupation with material things. The family in which both parents work is common. This has led to a gratifying increase in our standard of living but, in many cases, at a considerable sacrifice in family relations. It is difficult to communicate with a parent who isn't there or with one whose energy has been drained by the demands of a full-time job. It is equally difficult to supervise a youngster from the factory or, at the end of a long day, to resist the energy of a healthy teen-ager chafing at the bit.

Finally, consider the natural and necessary urge built into each youngster to rebel against adult authority, and it would seem to me that in many cases, we have provided a climate conducive to under-achievement.

The Rebels

Most experts agree that the most common cause of under-achievement is a conscious or unconscious rebellion against parental authority.

In guidance, we are interested primarily with "cures," not causes. However, if we acknowledge the existence of this rebellion in youngsters, some avenues leading to an improvement of the problem of under-achievement become apparent.

It would suggest, for instance, that punishment is probably not a feasible approach by a parent—or by a teacher. Punishment only results in increasing resentment and in stiffening the rebellion. Indeed, this has been the frustrating experience of so many parents with whom I have discussed this problem of under-achievement. By coincidence, this very day I was talking to a visiting alumnus who is enrolled in a prep school for a post-graduate year —a year made necessary by four years of classic under-achievement in high school. He is doing honor grade work at this time. However, I can remember remonstrating with his father who, in a desperate attempt to jolt him into action, had removed one privilege after another until the boy was permanently "grounded" and living a truly monastic existence. One might think that his reaction would have been to do what he so easily could have done—study his way out of it. But no, he ended the year by failing three subjects.

I'm not against discipline and punishment. I think they are very necessary to a child's training and sense of security. But one must be consistent, and to get tough suddenly in the senior year after 17 years of permissiveness simply won't work.

How should we handle such an under-achiever? I really don't know a universal formula, but I have some suggestions that might help. First, a few words to parents. Avoid putting pressure on the youngster by nagging him on his poor classroom performance. Accent the positive. Look for ways by which he *can* show his abilities and talents. Before he enters high school, give him some responsibilities and—if he carries them through—some freedom. Loosen the apron strings slowly but perceptibly. Spend some time with him. Let him feel that he is worthwhile, that you feel he is a *somebody*—not just a child. During the trying high school years, help him to establish a study routine—but again, don't nag him into studying. A firm but dispassionate policy is best and, for an anxious parent, the most difficult to maintain. Don't take away sports or other extra-curricular activities. We want him to like school—not to hate it! And these activities may be most important in giving him a feeling of worth and prestige among his classmates—a very necessary condition. Avoid criticizing him in front of his peers. Insofar as it is reasonable, support his teen-age image. Compromise where possible, but maintain firm rules of conduct. Do all this and you still may have an under-achiever, but it reduces the possibilities.

The Dissemblers

Some pupils are conscious under-achievers. These are the victims of their peer groups. Such a youngster finds that his academic talents are not particularly admired; in fact, they may become an obstacle to group acceptance. So he masks his ability by a delib-

erate under-achievement and becomes one of "the group." I wish
I had the answer to this one. I know one thing—the solution is *not*
an attempt to alienate him from his friends. A subtle program to
move him into activities that will bring him into contact with a
different group would be advantageous, but the chances are slim.
Group loyalties are absurdly strong. If the family can afford it,
such a youngster might be a candidate for a private school—which
is admitting defeat on the home grounds—but this has been a
realistic solution for a few fortunate ones.

The Immature

I have already voiced a pet theory—that many youngsters are
under-achievers because of their fear of not being able to measure
up to the demands of the adult world. For anyone who reads the
headlines, this is not difficult to understand. These kids are usually sensitive, immature, overly concerned with group acceptance
and dreamers. Again, although each child must be considered
separately, there are a few general rules that can be applied here.
The trick is to build up confidence, to mask irritation, and to avoid
harping on the obvious academic shortcomings of the youngster.
These kids are painfully aware of their deficiencies. Talk about the
necessity of a good education for a job or for college entrance
merely reinforces their sense of inadequacy. They need ego satisfaction—not lectures.

Parents, teachers and counselors can help by emphasizing positive aspects. If a student under-achieves, encourage him to take
steps to help himself. Avoid reinforcing the youngster's dissatisfaction with himself and with school. Never let him feel that you have
lost faith in him. Encourage him to talk or write about the things
he likes and does well. If it is possible, encourage him to enter a
school activity which might be the key to establishing his prestige
among his classmates.

These are all common tools of the elementary school teacher.
With our "cafeteria" style of high school education (it's there for
the student to get if he can), we sometimes overlook the simple
and basic techniques of "reaching" youngsters.

There is one practical measure that should be taken with any
under-achiever, but particularly with a student who suddenly
starts to perform at a lower level. A thorough physical, including

an eye and ear examination, is a highly desirable precaution. We occasionally spot youngsters who have a physical defect that has escaped the screening physical exams given in the school over the years. Or a defect may suddenly appear, as with the diabetic or the student with mononucleosis.

Despite all the procedures suggested above, certain youngsters will continue to under-achieve. I reiterate my conviction that the large majority of these young people will eventually come into their own. So patience, faith and affection are really the only ingredients that I can prescribe with any degree of confidence for the rather bitter pill that the parent and teacher must swallow. Mild sedatives occasionally help.

The disturbed child

My experience with severe cases of "disturbed" children has been quite meager. One reason, I suppose, is because a screening process has taken place over the years, and severely disturbed children seldom reach high school. However, we occasionally are faced with cases of mental illness, and so we should make some mention of the identification and handling of the problem.

My experience leads me to believe that identification of genuinely mentally ill children is usually not difficult. They exhibit extremes of behavior—extreme withdrawal, aggressiveness or anxiety, for example. Early symptoms are more subtle, but usually a teacher can spot a consistent departure from the norm. Naturally, I do not imply that we can be anything more than suspicious in these cases. It remains for a trained psychiatrist to diagnose a mental illness.

The next step is to bring the parents into the picture and convince them that we have reason to suspect serious trouble and to persuade them to arrange for a psychiatric evaluation. This gets easier every year. The old attitudes about mental illness are rapidly disappearing, and most parents accept the psychiatric clinic as readily as the hospital. Some still retain a deep prejudice and are most difficult to convince. This confrontation between parent and counselor is a difficult and delicate affair. We must avoid unduly alarming parents, but we must communicate our concern. It is important for us to remember that the responsibility for action belongs to the parent. They alone should make the referral.

I talk as though agencies for referral existed in every community. I'm not that naive. I know that many communities have no such services or, if they do, that they are overcrowded and working under severe difficulties. Part of a guidance program should consist of working towards the establishment of such a psychiatric service. We have recently established a child guidance clinic in our community. The initial steps were taken by members of the guidance staff, the school nurse, a local doctor and interested private citizens. It has proven a Godsend and has helped satisfy a long-felt need. The clinic is regional, supported by the state, the communities involved and by private contributions. This regional approach holds the greatest promise for successfully organizing and financing an effective clinic.

If there is one area that is in a critical need of expansion, it is this area of providing psychiatric services to the schoolchildren of communities. I suggest you forget teaching machines—let's get to work on this most urgent problem. We need more sociologists, psychologists and psychiatrists, and more money to implement the establishment and maintenance of these children's clinics. I believe guidance counselors can and should help create an awareness of this need in their communities.

If I seem to pass rather lightly over the problem of identification and handling of disturbed children, it is because I recognize my limitations. The reader should refer to a professional text on clinical psychology if he is interested in the details of symptoms, diagnosis and treatment. While I'm certainly interested, I cannot pose as an authority in this area, and so I am deliberately treating the problem from the point of view of the guidance counselor and emphasizing the limits of his involvement.

It seems to me that, as counselors, our function is to alert parents in cases of suspected illness that might require professional treatment, inform them of the possible sources of aid and assist them, if necessary, in securing such treatment for their children. Beyond this, our activities should be restricted to cooperating with the guidance clinics or whatever psychiatric service is involved. In addition, we can seek the advice of the professionals in charge of these cases as to how the school can best handle the youngster under treatment. But let's not play doctor at any stage of the game.

The rejected child

No counselor really knows what goes on in the homes of his counselees. I make a point of disbelieving half of what my clients say—until I find out differently. Still, one continually encounters the child who feels or actually *is* rejected by one or both parents. The victim of a broken home often feels rejected by at least one parent, and certainly has had a degree of security suddenly removed. A child with an alcoholic parent will feel rejected and insecure. Whether the rejection is real or fanciful matters little as far as their ultimate effect on the child is concerned. Of course, in the case of a child who is truly rejected, there is precious little we can do about changing the condition. We can't confront a parent and say "Hey, you—why don't you love your kid?" In fact, in so many similar problems stemming from home situations, we are helpless to change the basic facts of the case.

What can we do for these really unhappy kids? Not much, really. We can't change home conditions. We *can* provide friendship, trust and a place for them to "let down and cry." We can provide encouragement and the guidance missing at home. We can treat them as important individuals. And we can see to it that a sympathetic faculty is aware of the problem and reacts in a similar fashion. The total impact of these attitudes on a child is often surprisingly effective. The human spirit is remarkably tough and resilient. Sometimes it takes only one person in the entire school with whom the youngster can identify to make the difference between defeat and learning to live with the problem successfully. I have seen so many forlorn youngsters bloom in this atmosphere of friendliness that I can't help but think that all children, like puppies, respond to love—anybody's love.

These are the kids who are so vulnerable to teen-age romance. In an effort to find affection and security, they are too apt to give themselves blindly and prematurely to the first willing partner they can find. These are the youngsters who find themselves pregnant in the senior year—or much earlier.

I have often talked quite frankly to these emotionally-starved children who have obviously plunged into a highly emotional liaison. I try to point out their vulnerability and urge prudence and restraint. Maybe it has helped in some cases. In the absence of parental guidance, someone has to act *in loco parentis*. If the necessary rapport exists, I believe the counselor should try to help the child keep his or her emotional balance. Our success will depend on the degree of innate toughness of our young friends.

High school pregnancies

Statistics tell us that teen-age pregnancies are on the increase. This is probably true, although I can't see much difference in our community over twenty years. Be that as it may, it is always a disturbing experience for the counselor when it does happen. What should the counselor do when faced by a tear-stained youngster who has confessed to such a *fait accompli?*

My first rule is to do *nothing* without first bringing the parents into the picture. This is a highly personal *family* problem. We can so easily trespass on the rights of the family to handle their own affairs. Under certain circumstances, in the absence of any significant family guidance, I have pointed out the alternatives and possible courses of action. I have informed the youngsters as to the social agencies that might be of assistance and suggested in many occasions that they consult their pastor. But to make or even influence decisions such as whether to marry or to give up the child to an agency is to assume an authority that the counselor does not have. At the very most, I have talked to the young couple, at their request, about the situation. We have discussed the responsibilities of marriage, their readiness and maturity and certain practical aspects of earning a living, etc. I adhere rigidly to an impersonal exposition of facts and avoid influencing a decision—at least, I try to. It's very difficult when one feels strongly about a situation. As with most guidance problems, the task of maintaining a position midway between strongly influencing the couple in an attempt to forestall what might appear to us to be a tragic mistake and of maintaining a completely impersonal attitude is difficult as a general rule. I suggest that we tend to stay away from attempts to influence. Again I say that this is a highly personal problem. If we were the parents we would have the right to say whatever we wanted. As counselors, we are constrained to hold our tongues. All we can do is to make sure the youngsters are informed of the alternative courses of action and the possible consequences of each course.

If this sounds heartless, I must confess that on a few rare occasions I have ignored my own advice and have quite openly suggested what seemed to me to be the only course of action to take. The fact that in these cases there was an almost complete lack of parental concern does not completely exonerate me. I might have been wrong. However, mine was the only mature advice available. But it comes pretty close to playing God, you know.

I have a few suggestions for the new counselor that will prepare him for such pregnancies. First, get acquainted with the pastors of the churches in your community. This is good guidance practice in any event, but the clergy are very valuable for referral in these cases. Next, determine the social agencies that can help—homes for unwed mothers, sources of financial help for the family—sources of obstetrical assistance and the like. Thus informed, you may be able to help families who are ignorant or overwhelmed.

Finally, the counselor can aid in arranging for the continued education of the youngsters involved or in locating jobs for the young father if the situation demands it. Throughout the whole procedure, the youngsters should feel that they are welcome to discuss their problems, to seek help and information. We may not be able to make their decisions for them, but we can insure that they have as much information as possible with which to arrive at a solution to their dilemma.

Sample case studies

Let's look at some actual problem cases typical of those one might encounter in any school. I have two purposes in mind: to illustrate some of the preceding philosophy and to provide the reader an opportunity to try his hand at unravelling some of the tangles that trap our youngsters. I have masked the identities of the cases but, beyond changing minor details, the essential elements remain as they are. I will pose the problem and suggest that the reader work out his solution, and then compare it with the action that was actually taken. As with most problems of mankind, there is no one solution, and for some of these cases the handling was far from successful as it turned out.

I. The Case of "Cool Kenny."

Kenny burst on the scene as an ebullient sophomore, outgoing, brash and loudly vocal. A good junior high record and his I.Q. score of 125 and above testifies to a superior mind, as did his ready wit. His family was well to do, obviously concerned for the boy. The mother was gentle and sweet—no match for Kenny. The father was more of sterner stuff, but was on the road much of the time. A younger sister was doing well in junior high.

The problem originated early in the sophomore year. As Kenny's hormones took over, his achievement plummeted. His natural ability saw him through the sophomore year. By mid-term of his junior year, Kenny was riding high, bombing around town on secondhand wheels, a real groovy guy, but look at his record:

9th Grade		10th Grade	
(Junior High)			
English 1	A	English 2C	B
Geography	B	World History 2C	D
Gen. Science	A	Biology	D
Algebra 1	B	Geometry	C
Latin 1	C	Latin 2 (dropped)	E
Phys. Ed.	C	Phys. Ed.	D

11th Grade

	FIRST TERM	MID YEAR
English 3C	C	D
U.S. History	D	D
Chemistry	D	E
Algebra 2	C	D
Spanish 1	D	E
Phys. Ed.	D	D

Faced with demanding courses, Kenny's unwillingness to study proved disastrous. His family was frantic, his teachers perplexed. Obviously something had to be done. What would you—as counselor—do in this situation? The actual denouement appears at the end of this section. (Just like Perry Mason? Maybe we should insert a commercial here. A headache panacea might be appropriate.)

II. The Case of the "Unwed Mother."

I got to know Sandy in her junior year. Her mother was recently divorced and already interested in another gentleman. Sandy's sense of security was threatened by a divided loyalty to both parents. She needed an adult to confide in, and I served as a sort of foster father during school hours. She was a pretty, intelligent girl who did rather well academically in spite of the home situation. She was accepted by a state teacher's college in her senior year and I was very pleased with the whole situation.

My smugness was shot to pieces when she sought me out in April and in a tearful confession, informed me that she was pregnant. I quickly ascertained that both sets of parents were aware of the fact and that Sandy's mother, though badly shaken, was ready to help her in any way.

The problem appeared to be whether Sandy should get married or not. She claimed to be genuinely in love with the boy—also a senior from a nearby community. She couldn't get him to commit himself one way or another. She showed a surprising maturity in that she was apparently ready to accept the fact that he might not be ready for marriage. But it was this uncertainty, together with feelings of guilt and betrayal, that was seriously upsetting her. So she came to me, her only adult male confidant, for help. What would *you* have done?

III. The Case of the "Discarded Daughter."

There's something about the junior year that uncovers situations previously undetected. Maybe it's because by then the youngsters feel they know you well enough to confide in you. Maybe it's because the students are growing up and are more sensitive to adult feelings and reactions. At any rate, it was late in her junior year when Mary broke down in my office. Her grandmother had recently died. She had never known her father. Her older brother was in the service, and her mother hated her! I took this last with a grain of salt but, as it turned out, it was not overstated.

Mary was a pretty, intelligent girl, but her marks had slipped badly. She was getting sloppy about her grooming and told me she had been drinking regularly. She wanted and needed her mother desperately, but her mother obviously did not want her. Mary was on the verge of an emotional breakdown.

Mary did not want me to talk with the mother, so I verified the story through a former friend who had been a neighbor of the family and who had employed Mary as a baby sitter. The home situation was indeed intolerable. What to do?

IV. The Case of the "Sad Sophomore."

Jenny was indeed a pathetic creature. At fourteen and a sophomore, she had a figure as shapely as a knotted rope—5 feet tall, 98 pounds—and with a plain, bony face that prompted unkind classmates to dub her "Auntie" Jenny. She had no friends, depended on her family for affection. Endowed with a low average scholastic aptitude, she was doing very poorly in general courses when she saw me in the fall.

Her answer to my questioning was to burst into tears and recount the most revealing and heartrending recital of personal troubles that I have heard before or since. She was afraid of school. Having known nothing but failure in the adolescent world, she expected nothing but failure for herself in any endeavor. She was acutely aware of her physical shortcomings and ashamed of her inability to live up to her parents' hopes. Most of all, she was desperately lonely. She needed someone outside the family for a friend. The floor was soggy with Kleenex when she finally finished her tale of woe. I confess I was somewhat "shook up" myself. She certainly posed quite a problem. Could anything be done?

V. The Case of the "Blind Boy."

Bill came to us practically unannounced. He had concluded several years of training at a school for the blind and was entering his sophomore year in our public high school. The prospect of supervising the education of a blind boy was somewhat overwhelming. As it turned out, our fears were totally unfounded in Bill's case.

Our first intimation as to Bill's self-sufficiency and excellent mind came his first day of school when we introduced him to his algebra class. The teacher, in an effort to make him feel at home, described the particular problem on the board and then asked the class for the solution. Bill put up his hand without hesitation and provided the correct answer.

Later we took him around the building to help him learn the location of his classes, the library, gym, etc. His ability to remember was uncanny. After one trip, Bill was practically on his own. Despite Bill's self-sufficiency, however, we were still faced with a few problems. If he couldn't read, how could he study? He couldn't take notes. How to bring the printed page to his searching, brilliant mind? These questions, and others, provided us with quite a problem.

SOLUTIONS (?) TO CASES

Case I. "Cool Kenny."

A council of war was held with Kenny's parents. Out of this emerged a five-point program:

1. His evening activities during the school week were limited to occasional school-sponsored activities—basketball games, Hi-Y meetings, etc. This was not done in an attempt to punish, but as a logical and necessary action to provide needed study time.

2. Kenny worked out his own study schedule in such a way as to provide adequate study time and still allow a reasonable freedom to do the things that were important to him.

3. A biweekly "Report of Progress" form was initiated. This provided Kenny and his family a regular report on his performance—a report which promoted a realistic awareness on Kenny's part.

4. Regular help sessions with the chemistry teacher were initiated. Spanish appeared to be a losing battle—he just hadn't learned enough in the first two terms. He dropped it and took college typing in its place (a half-year course).

5. We arranged for a student tutor to work with him on algebra during study hall for a few weeks.

Result? I wish I could report that Kenny's record showed dramatic improvement. It didn't, they seldom do! But he did show some progress, and his final marks were as follows:

English 3C	C D C C	Final C
U.S. History	D D D C	Final D
Chemistry	D *E* D D	Final D
Algebra	C D C C	Final C
Spanish	D *E* (dropped)	
College Typing	C C	Final C

He worked that summer in the factory of a family friend. This was an invaluable experience. He did well enough in his senior year to be accepted by a community college. He eventually transferred to a state college where he did superior work. He is a successful business and family man at this time.

Conclusion: Kenny—the classic under-achiever—fared about as well as could be expected. We have found no miraculous cures for the "Kenny's." But his parents' patience under extreme pressure eventually paid off. Kenny might have ended up hating school, a typical rebel. His parents wisely left him a necessary amount of freedom as they tightened their control.

Had they applied tighter controls earlier would Kenny still have under-achieved? I think so—to a degree, at least. Our society offers too many distractions to a boy like Kenny—distractions that have far more appeal to a high school junior than do the disciplines of study.

However, if we can keep from hitting the panic button, most of these frustrating cases will have a happy ending.

Case II. "The Unwed Mother."

Faced by an outright plea for help, I first suggested that Sandy talk with the parish priest, but she didn't feel she knew him well enough. That left me as the only one in whom she could confide. Not that I didn't want to help—I just hesitate to interfere. We decided it was time that some neutral party talked to Eddie, the boy friend, in an attempt to clarify the situation. Sandy persuaded him to come in after school, and we had a long man-to-man talk.

It soon became apparent that though he was genuinely fond of Sandy, he was in no way ready for marriage, emotionally or financially. Under the circumstances it would have been courting an even greater disaster for anyone to have encouraged such a marriage.

However, the choice was still theirs. I heard Eddie out, asked a few questions, pointed out a few facts and avoided any advice or opinion beyond the fact that he owed Sandy a decision based on an honest self-evaluation. I think the mere fact that I did not immediately assume he would marry the girl was helpful in his self-analysis. At any rate, he told Sandy how he felt, and they decided not to get married. She finished high school, gave up the baby to an agency and entered college a year later.

Conclusion: One could hardly call this a solution. Lord knows what emotional scars an experience like this will leave on them! However, note that the role of the counselor was not to give advice, but to help them reach a very difficult decision based on a realistic self-appraisal. They might have decided to get married. Had they done so, they might be very happy now. I doubt it—the cards were stacked against them. The important thing to remember in these cases is that it must be their decision—not ours.

Case III. *"The Discarded Daughter."*

After some investigating and a few more sessions with Mary, I decided immediate steps should be taken. I called her minister—with her consent, of course—and arranged for an early consultation. I related the story to him. He was somewhat aware of the home situation and most sympathetic. He agreed to act as a "go between" in order to place Mary in the home of one of his parishioners. He also volunteered to see Mary often in the near future in an attempt to help her over the present emotional crisis. As it turned out, after talking with the minister, I called Mary's former neighbor on a hunch. I outlined the situation, and the upshot was that Mary spent the rest of that year and the next with her as part of her family. I also enlisted the aid of a local doctor, a wonderfully warm and understanding woman who had been most helpful in working with some of our "problem" girls in the past. She saw Mary periodically that spring and attempted to help her accept the fact of the mother's rejection.

Mary graduated, worked for a while and was married the next fall. I hope she eventually outlives the scars of the traumatic period that nearly destroyed her.

Conclusion: It is obvious that the help afforded by the counselor in this case was of a practical nature—to provide a stable home environment—not to attempt psychotherapy. I left this up to more expert hands. This case is an example of how community "specialists" can assist the guidance program. I might add that I did contact the appropriate state agency. They were sympathetic but bogged down with a backlog of cases. I have found that church leaders are most cooperative and effective in crisis situations like the above. We have one or two cases a year that we would like to place in such homes. Often, when you need a foster home, you need it immediately. I have urged that our council of churches develop a list of cooperating families that are willing to provide a temporary home for a senior until she can achieve some independence.

Of course there are certain legal considerations in these cases involving foster homes. In this state, for instance, court action or written consent of the parents is necessary to provide the foster parents with custodial powers and legal protection.

Case IV. "The Sad Sophomore."

The first thing I did was to wipe Jenny's red nose for her. The second thing I did was to adopt her as my school-time daughter. Oh yes, we talked about her courses and I tried to bolster her confidence. We worked together on history every other week or so. I made a point of seeing her as often as possible on one pretext or another. She dropped in from time to time on her own, mostly when she was apprehensive of her academic progress.

Meanwhile, a conference with her mother assured me that she had no particular medical problem and that her family was doing everything they could to provide an atmosphere of affection and security.

Jenny scraped by her sophomore and junior years. Progress in building her self-confidence was slow. Tears flowed less frequently, but there were many times when I was tempted to rig the scenario and arrange for her to be taken into the "in" group. And when she was a senior and wanted so badly to go to her first (and last) school dance, I was so close to breaking all my own rules. I almost called in a dateless senior boy—a kind, thoughtful kid—to ask him to take her. He would have, too. But I resisted the temptation. I might have been wrong, but I refuse to play games— even well-meant games—with people's lives.

I saw Jenny regularly throughout her last two years of high school. She decided she wanted to be a practical nurse in her junior year. I was none too optimistic, although I didn't say so. However, I did point out the requirements and the necessity for improving her grades which were mostly "D's." She did much better in her senior year, but not well enough to be admitted. However, we had already planned on a post-graduate year if necessary. So Jenny came back, took algebra and biology and did well enough to be admitted to the mid-year class. This was a moment of mutual triumph. I breathed a gusty sigh of relief.

Jenny returned to see me after she had been capped. As I looked at this self-possessed young lady, it was hard to envision the forlorn waif of three years ago. She was well groomed, almost pretty—she *was* pretty—glowing with well-justified pride. I have never felt such satisfaction in my job as I did at that moment!

Conclusion: Love indeed accomplishes miracles. If we can give little else, we can still justify our profession. Lest the reader feel I am claiming too much credit for myself, let me assure you that I know better. I happened to be there when she needed a friend. I have seen this relationship between my colleagues and certain of their counselees grow in the same way. It is the most important service we can provide our troubled youngsters—it is often the *only* service we can provide them. To be a friend, to show faith and trust—this is to be a counselor. And when that faith and trust is reciprocated—that's what makes counseling worthwhile.

Case V. "The Blind Boy."

Bill's case serves as another example of community involvement and the use of outside agencies. One of the first things Bill's counselor did was to contact the Local Junior Volunteer Service of the local Women's Club. Through this organization, a team of readers was formed to provide Bill with a regular reading service during his study hall time. The Massachusetts State Division of the Blind was exceedingly cooperative. Through their office, we secured a copy of a brochure dealing with the education of the blind. This excellent booklet included guidelines for teachers, lists of suggested teaching materials and equipment and a list of agencies concerned with the blind. Through the Division we were able to secure records and books. The Library of Congress was able to furnish brailled textbooks. A volunteer worker in a nearby community did additional brailling. A local industry contributed a small portable tape recorder. A representative of the Division of Rehabilitation (blind himself) made regular visits to advise us and evaluate Bill's progress in gaining control of his environment. A volunteer from a church agency visited from Boston to give Bill instruction in ambulation downtown and around his neighborhood.

It was heartening to discover the wealth of material already available. It was equally heart-warming to find the agencies and volunteer individuals so willing to give their time.

With his excellent mind and aggressive spirit, Bill did exceedingly well in school and on his college boards (voluntarily administered by Springfield College). He was accepted by an excellent college where he continued to do superior work.

Conclusion: Whereas we should not take credit for Bill's success, a large amount of work and time was spent by his counselor in lining up the personnel and materials for his course of study. Without the availability of state and local organizations and individuals, it would have been an impossible task. But it can be done —as we proved to our mild surprise—by using all the help available.

12

Planning for the Future

It may indeed be true that society can't have its cake and eat it too. Most of us are living in an environment of unparalleled affluence. Yet we are plagued with a slow erosion of national morality coupled with a rising surge of teen-age delinquency and rebellion—and this among middle class America. History abounds with parallel situations, and it behooves us to heed the voices of the past lest we also succumb to the weakness of man's insatiable appetite for self-indulgence.

How did we get this way? There are many obvious answers—from political attempts to find quick, easy solutions of problems to the disturbing reality that too many people have everything except convictions. This national confusion is reinforced by the fault that we are the beneficiaries of a questionable educational inheritance—namely the permissive philosophy of a generation ago.

I have referred to our permissive society in the past. I would like to explore the phenomenon further in an attempt to relate the role of society, the parent and the counselor in the face of what appears to be an impending social crisis.

An unfortunate legacy

Many of the educational weaknesses of today were innocently introduced in the early 1900's. Prodded by John Dewey and company, many educators became justifiably concerned with the traditional, ultra-conservative, often dull pedagogy that characterized the schools of that period. In an attempt to stimulate individual growth and relate learning experiences to life, a new emphasis on the individual was introduced. The concept of the "child-centered" school was born. Education has benefited in large measure from all this.

This was also during the period when psychology reared its head and society became bemused with Freud, self-expression, inhibitions, egos, ids and the world of the subconscious. Somehow, the academic pendulum swung a little too far to the left, Dewey's ideas were distorted, and we were sold the idea that kids were really tiny adults—capable of making wise decisions if allowed. And so the classroom was turned into a kind of exploratory test tube with the teacher assuming a minor role as guide and fellow-playmate while the children ran the show. School became a veritable beehive of activities run by student committees with little interference from teacher or principal.

The results were regrettable. Armed with the assurance that freedom for self-expression was necessary for the child's development, educators removed the discipline and work from the curriculum. Once the concept of the child-centered school was accepted, the authority of the teacher was diminished. The sandbox replaced the multiplication table and the class committee replaced the teacher. American schools became socially rather than academically oriented. Even now the school is often a social rather than an educational agency.

Eventually the pendulum swung back as common sense took over. As to be expected, much good came from this period and our classrooms are livelier, our students better motivated, our teachers more skillful because of it. But irreparable harm has been

done. Our society still is a permissive society, even if our classrooms are not.

More subtle effects can be discerned. In an attempt to make
learning a "democratic process," a protective mantle was cast over
the children. In an effort to avoid the traumatic effects of academic
failure and to cater to the "whole child," scholastic competition
was de-emphasized and social activities encouraged. The result,
painfully evident today, is the lack of prestige afforded the brilliant student, while the school athlete receives the accolades of
both his peers and of society in general. There is, indeed, a general distrust of the "egghead" even in our adult society. The "well-
rounded" college man is far more acceptable than the sharper, and
more uncomfortable, intellectual.

Another facet of the permissive philosophy that persists today
is that everything has to be fun. I have nothing against the idea
that school should be fun—I think it can and should be. But, unfortunately, someone confused the concept of fun with the word
"easy." Even now I read publishers' descriptions of textbooks
that advertise *Geometry Made Easy* and similar siren songs. How
about *Calculus for the Mental Defective* or *Leisure-time Latin?*
Even today our students have been conditioned to expect entertainment, not enlightenment. I do not recomend a return to the
little red schoolhouse, but I think we can expect a degree of discipline and effort from our students at every level.

Even as I write this I am aware of the fact that many of our
students are working harder and progressing further than their
parents ever did. But these students are a minority group in the
average school. Most children are not sufficiently challenged to
perform at their academic potential. I'm afraid that for many
children, the academic route is still the primrose path.

The age of disillusionment

Adolescence has always been a period of idealism—a time for
questioning adult values. Today's communication media, however, make it difficult for the teen-ager to reconcile what he is
taught with what he sees going on around him. He is painfully
aware of graft or unethical practices within the ranks of our country's leaders. He reads, for instance, that a giant corporation is
fined for price-fixing. He sees that a respected lawyer in town is

under indictment for failure to truthfully report income. His father brags of fixing a traffic ticket and his sister wears a padded bra. If this is what the young idealists encounter as they open their eyes to the formidable adult world they are about to enter, it is no wonder that many are disillusioned. If they are to withstand the shock, they need the support of an authoritarian background both in the home and in the school. Because they are inexperienced and ignorant of life, they need to be told what is right and wrong—of having limits firmly defined. Moreover, parents and teachers must interpret an imperfect world in such a way as to make it acceptable to impatient and critical youngsters.

Our children must have known discipline and denial. How can we expect our youngsters to take any other than the easy road if they have known no other? Without the support of a family, school and community consensus as to what is intelligent, good and right, our young people will fall easy prey to the lotus eaters.

The Role of Society

There seems to be a tendency in our society to overemphasize teen-age culture. It's almost as though society is saying "If you can't beat 'em, join 'em." Certainly one sees abundant evidence of an attempt to perpetuate adolescence. Many radio stations pander to teen-age tastes almost exclusively. Movies and TV offer an endless parade of shallow, immature and adolescent entertainment. The clothing industry has grown fat on the development of teen-age fads and fashions.

Although it is obviously exaggerated, I agree somewhat with the Hechingers' viewpoint of today's high school society as portrayed in their book *Teen-Age Tyranny.*[1] "Instead of making adolescence a transition period, necessary and potentially even valuable (if often slightly comical), it (the American society) began to turn it into a separate way of life to be catered to, exaggerated, and extended far beyond its biological duration."

It is high time for society to look upon teen-agers as kids growing up—not as some kind of social club—a club with special privi-

---

[1] Grace and Fred M. Hechinger, *Teen-Age Tyranny* (Greenwich, Connecticut: Fawcett Publications).

leges whose members are exempt from the usual responsibilities and penalties of adult life.

Society would do well to look for ways by which it can give teen-agers responsibility and permit them a greater involvement with real life. It has been my experience that when youngsters are given an opportunity as a group to shoulder responsibility, they have carried it off with flying colors. I'm thinking of the kids who volunteered as counselors for our summer camp for the mentally retarded; of the boys and girls who took part in the tag day for the blind; of the green girls in the hospital; of the tremendous interest in the appeal of the Peace Corps and Vista. There are too few opportunities for this kind of involvement in modern society.

The Role of the Parent

Because I am a parent, I realize as much as anyone the difficulty of prescribing a course of action for parents in dealing with their children. It's a case of the blind leading the blind. We are all inflicted with a peculiar astigmatism when it comes to our own kids.

Nevertheless, the key to the problem of developing a productive responsible teen-age society lies in the hands of the parent, and in no other agency.

As I have said before, ours is a rather conservative town. Yet I am appalled at the apparent lack of concern exhibited by parents as to the activities and whereabouts of their children. Too many of our youngsters drink, not just occasionally, experimentally, but regularly, as dictated by the mores of an admittedly small segment of the group. I find it hard to believe that their parents approve. I find it equally hard to believe that the parents are ignorant of their children's nocturnal activities. What, then, is the answer?

Are parents really afraid of them? Or are parents fearful of admitting to themselves that their offspring are the result of their own failure as parents? Do they, as do adolescents, live in a dream world, fearful of facing reality, afraid to probe lest they uncover unwelcome facts? Or do they just want to be pals to their children—good, understanding buddies who want to be admitted to the adolescent world on adolescent terms?

A few parents really don't give a damn. I'm not talking about them. These are sick people who are in the minority in most average communities. No, I'm talking about the nice couple across any street who will open their home for a teen-age party and then leave for the movies. Or the family that gives a beer party for members of the graduating class. Or the hundreds of god-fearing mothers and fathers who go to bed night after night, not knowing where their adolescent offspring are or what they are doing. Faith is fine, but this is ridiculous.

Eventually our young men and women must make their personal decisions regarding sex, alcohol or drugs. I don't think for one minute that they have the maturity to make this decision as adolescents. Some may argue that only a few months separate the high school senior from the college freshman. Why then should the senior be denied the freedom that the freshman enjoys? One reason is that the senior is still in high school and his actions will color the behavior of those in his own class, as well as the precocious underclassmen who are eager to establish themselves as really mature cool cats. I might also add that obviously not all college freshmen are in a position to make the same decisions with mature judgment. Certainly being in college does not automatically endow them with wisdom and maturity.

The inescapable fact is that high school students are *not* capable of handling themselves in an adult fashion. They *cannot* handle the problems of drinking or sex if given a free hand. But complete freedom forces them to face these problems before they are ready. They need the assistance of a more rigidly controlled society, wherein the parents call the shots. It makes me glow all over to hear a parent say to his son, "I don't care when Lennie and Bob are supposed to be home; you be here by eleven or else!" That type of control takes courage, but it is necessary!

Only a childhood of reasonable discipline and denial, backed up by the example of moderate, sensible parents will provide the young man or woman with the conditioning necessary to make intelligent choices. And we must start when they're in diapers. Today is too late.

I suggest that we expect too much of our youngsters in some areas and not enough in others. We expect them to be able to discipline themselves when observation and experience tells us otherwise. We give them too much freedom in the naive expectation that they will use it wisely. Few adolescents are capable of handling the leisure time they have nor the mobility of today's high school society. In five minutes, the car can swoop them far, far away from the inhibitive influence of their own neighborhood. There, on the other side of town, protected by anonymity, spurred by boredom, bolstered by the group and inspired by their own youthful imagination, anything can happen.

At the same time, we have a right to expect courtesy and respect. TV commercials bother me as they must everyone, but commercials which feature sulky, rude and impertinent kids only reinforce a feeling in parents that this is normal and to be expected. We forgive our youngsters too much in the name of adolescence. Granted that this is a trying experience, we are doing them no favor by *letting* them act like young children. We are not encouraging self-sufficiency if we don't give them responsibility—and at an early age.

I suggest we give our children too much. How can they practice self-denial? I suggest we are too permissive. How can we expect them to develop self-discipline? It is difficult, in an affluent society, to do differently. But we should try, from the time they are in diapers till the time we put them on the train for state college.

I hope I don't sound too smug. I feel I've earned the right to do a *little* preaching. You see, I've made all the mistakes most other well-meaning parents make. Of course, I've been luckier than most, probably because my eldest takes after her mother.

May I offer the following ten commandments for the guidance of parents who love their children? And I do this with humility and an acute awareness that no man—not even Dr. Spock—knows all the answers.

    I. Thou shalt not shower thy offspring with filthy lucre to purchase their affection—nor give gifts, nor ice cream sodas in unseemly quantities.

   II. Thou shalt not spare the hairbrush for thy young, nor the thunder of thy displeasure at thy stripling.

  III. Thou shalt not lend the tribal chariot without prudence but sparingly and for excellent purpose.

   IV. Thou shalt set before thy sons and daughters tasks to perform that they might grow in wisdom and self-esteem.

   V. Thou shalt shear the locks of thy sons and lengthen the hems of thy daughters that all men may tell them apart and find them innocent.

   VI. Thou shalt lie awake, awaiting the return of the prodigal, that ye may mark his progress and set his feet upon the paths of righteousness.

   VII. Thou shalt give richly of thy time that thy children are comforted and not alone.

   VIII. Thou shalt frequently say nay with stout heart and steadfast mind but be not too craven to occasionally say yea.

   IX. Thou shalt cherish the flesh of thy flesh, fearing not to *display* thy affection.

   X. Thou shalt have faith in the Lord.

I think there is a message there even though it is admittedly rightwing.

The Role of the Counselor

My conception of the role of the counselor is based on the following assumptions.

1. *Teenagers are ignorant*. They are ignorant of life because they haven't lived long enough.

2. *They are afraid of becoming adults*. They doubt their ability to assume the adult role, vocationally, socially and sexually. Consequently, they seek refuge in their own private society.

3. *Teen-agers need the security of an authoritative environment*. Both at home, in school and in the neighborhood. They will scream in an agony of protest and rebellion against any encroachment on their "rights." But, deep down, they want and need restraints.

4. *Teen-agers are idealists*.

If these statements are true, as I think they are, certain conclusions follow.

Because high school youngsters are ignorant of life, it follows that the counselor, with his superior experience and knowledge, is justified in a directive approach to counseling in many situations.

School and occupational choice, selection of and adjustment to an individual's program of courses are examples of the decisions which, based as they are on factual considerations, should be directly influenced by the counselor. I find that most experienced counselors become progressively less and less Rogerian with each passing year, insofar as the planned program is concerned.

Because the teen-ager is fearful of adulthood, he is in constant need of encouragement and assurance. In this instance, the counselor assumes a supportive role. As an adult in a neutral corner of the youngster's world, he can act as an ally against the threats of adulthood and an interpreter of adults and the adult establishment. He can help the youngster envision himself in an adult role and show him practical ways of entering the world of grown-ups.

Because teen-agers need the security of authority, the counselor should assume an attitude that will support the authority of the family, school and society.

Because teen-agers are idealists, the counselor should be scrupulously honest and straightforward in his dealings with his counselees. While the children of this generation may doubt adult values, the one thing they look for and respect is honesty. They meet up with so much double talk! They are masters of spotting the phony. At the same time, all youngsters respond to honesty and trust.

Finally, because teen-agers are really people, not "TEEN-AGERS," they, like all people at all ages, need to be loved. This is the counselor's most precious gift. I hope we all have an adequate supply.

Thus the counselor becomes an ally of the developing adolescent, a source of information that will help unlock the doors to adulthood, an advocate of authority and an interpreter of reality. He is a foster father without portfolio and, as such, he offers no threat to the wary teen-ager. He is understanding but not permissive. And he is deeply concerned with every one of his counselees.

Conclusion

At the start of this book, I promised a point of view which I advertised as sensible guidance. I fervently hope I have stated my case with clarity and conviction. If I have dwelt overlong on the limitations of guidance, forgive me, but it was done purposely.

If the preceding chapters have held a message it is that as counselors we can do certain things well. But there are other areas we should not invade. In the area of the planned program, we are on solid—if traditional—ground. When we trespass on the province of the psychiatrist, we are courting failure. We are equipped to advise on schools, jobs, school courses and the like, but we are playing at God when we try to influence highly personal decisions. As with so many problems in life, there is a middle course which avoids the granite rigidity of authority and the quicksands of permissiveness.

There is no question in my mind but that guidance is here to stay. It is not an educational fad. It has great potential as an auxiliary service which will make the total educational process more effective. It insures that the individual will not be overlooked in an era when the individual threatens to be buried by the sheer weight of numbers. Guidance is our best hope for the development of individualism during the adolescent years.

I hope that many enthusiastic, courageous, humble and patient young people are attracted to the field. I can attest to its challenging, stimulating and rewarding qualities. As a final inducement, I can assure the reader that, over the years, I have laughed more than I have cried.

Last September while interviewing freshmen I met the daughter of one of my former students. (It is happening with alarming frequency now.) She looked at me out of shining blue eyes and said, "Mother wanted me to say 'Hi' to you. She says she'll always remember you. She says you were the only one who paid any attention to her."

The defense rests.

Index